RUNNING A WORKSHOP

Basic business for craftspeople

CONTRIBUTORS

Tony Ford
Amanda Hare
David Kay
Morris Latham
Liz Lydiate
Barclay Price

EDITED BY *Barclay Price*

Revised edition 1989

ISBN 0 903798 80 8

Published by the Crafts Council
12 Waterloo Place
London SW1Y 4AU

Designed by Philip Miles

Printed in Great Britain
by Gaffyne & Brown Ltd

CONTENTS

FOREWORD

Research by the Crafts Council has shown that craftsmen and women have earnings well below the national average and that their major worries are about business problems, especially selling their work. In response the Crafts Council produced *Running A Workshop*, of which this is a revised edition, and to date the book has sold over 4,000 copies, thereby underlining the demand for such advice. No book can hope to be a complete guide to setting up and running a workshop, but we think that we have covered the problems at least in enough detail to warn the reader of pitfalls ahead and to point out where to go for further advice.

We realise that craftspeople do not wish to become multi-national corporations but most are interested in seeing their work sold and in getting a fair return for their efforts, but to survive in the market place they must understand basic commercial principles. What this book aims to do, therefore, is to give straightforward advice and information relevant to the small size of most craft businesses. As a result, we hope such businesses will run more effectively, and make more profit.

It is encouraging that recent research into craftspeople supported by the Crafts Council has shown that around 70% are still successfully running their craft businesses after ten years, a remarkably high percentage for small businesses and an indication that the market for contemporary crafts continues to grow. The sales of crafts within this country and abroad are beginning to form a significant slice of the economy. We hope that readers of this book will be encouraged to join the growing number of crafts businesses.

Running A Workshop has been produced by Crafts Council staff. A set of two videos linked to the book is also available. These include interviews with individual craftspeople and working examples of some of the points contained within the book. Further information on crafts and craft businesses in England and Wales is obtainable from the Crafts Council.

Tony Ford
Director, Crafts Council
1989

INTRODUCTION

Whatever your reasons for wanting to set up as a maker, it is important to realise that a career in crafts tends to involve long working hours for little money; like all new small businesses, you will need to be determined if you are to survive the normally difficult initial years.

Before going any further, you must sit down and look at the potential for your work. It may well be worth spending some time in an established workshop where you will gain valuable insights into the realities of working in crafts. At the very least, talk to a number of craftsmen and women about their experiences. It is also useful to talk over your plans with friends and relations whose views you trust and respect, before committing yourself.

Given the ups and down experienced by everyone setting up in business on their own, it helps to write down a list of your objectives, *realistic* objectives: having a lot of exhibitions is not enough in itself if you sell nothing and are forced out of business. Everyone's objectives will be different; one craftsperson may plan to have an annual turnover of £15,000 after two years, own a house and workshop in the country and sell through ten outlets, while another hopes to achieve a £30,000 turnover, be featured in a national magazine and work mainly to commission. Different objectives will necessitate different approaches, and you can refer to your list as a guide before deciding on your next step. By periodically matching reality against your original objectives, you will be able to assess your relative success or failure without allowing your judgement to be coloured too much by either depression or temporary euphoria.

MONEY

Whether you are just starting up or are already operating a craft workshop, it is fairly certain that you will require some capital.

If you are starting up, you will need money to rent premises, buy equipment and materials, and see you through the initial months before cash from sales starts to come in. You must ensure that you have enough cash to support yourself through this period.

Even if you have been running your workshop for a time and have an income from sales, it is likely that at some point you will require extra funds to buy bulk materials for stock, to allow you to build up work for an exhibition, or to replace or buy new equipment. Unless you are fortunate enough to have sufficient resources of your own, you will need to obtain funding from elsewhere, which means applying for a grant or borrowing.

GRANTS

Only a few schemes are detailed as what is on offer tends to change from time to time. Best to check with relevant bodies to obtain information on their current schemes.

Crafts Council
01 930 4811
(England and Wales only)

Setting Up Scheme
Maintenance grant of £2200 for one year and 50% of the cost of essential equipment to assist with setting up a first workshop. Applicants must be within two years of setting up.

Department of Employment
Contact local Job Centre

Enterprise Allowance Scheme
Available to those starting a business who have been out of work for at least 8 weeks and are receiving either Unemployment or Supplementary Benefit at the time of applying. A grant of £40 per week is paid.

Scottish Development Agency (Crafts Division)
031 337 9595
(Scotland except Highlands & Islands)

The Crafts Setting Up Scheme
Maintenance grant of up to £2000 in first year and 50% of cost of essential equipment and/or renovation of workshop premises, to a maximum of £1,000. *Workshop & Equipment Scheme* Grants of up to 50% of cost of an approved programme of development, designed to raise standards of production and increase output. Maximum grant £2,000. *Start Up Workshop & Equipment Scheme* Grant of up to 50% of cost of establishing a full-time crafts workshop. Maximum grant £1,000.

Regional Arts Associations
See Pages 125/126 for regions and addresses
(England and Wales)

Some Regional Arts Associations offer small grants to individual craftspeople.

Local Enterprise Development Unit
0232 242582
(Northern Ireland only)

Rural Development Commission
(formerly) Council for Small Industries in Rural Areas
Ring 0722 336255 for details of local offices.

(Rural areas of England and country towns with populations of up to 10,000)

Mid-Wales Development
0686 26965
(Mid Wales only)

Welsh Development Agency
044 385 2666
(Rural areas of Wales)

Welsh Craft Initiative
0248 370082 (North Wales)
0686 626965 (Mid Wales)
0792 561666 (South & West Wales)

Highlands & Islands Development Board
0463 244382
(Scottish highlands & islands)

London Enterprise Agency
01 236 3000
(London only)

Small Firms Service

This is an advisory service offering assistance in setting up and running a business. Information in response to enquiries with up to three sessions of free counselling for more complicated matters.
For your nearest office dial 100 and ask for Freefone Enterprise.

Other Enterprise Agencies/Local Council Development Agencies

No detailed information. However a number of schemes are available throughout the country so check with your local council to see if there are local schemes relevant to your business.

Trusts
(Consult "Directory of Grant-Making Trusts" in your reference library)

Some charitable trusts offer support to those starting up craft business, although the number is limited. *The Princes Trust* has supported a number of younger craftspeople with grants for equipment.

Winston Churchill Memorial Trust

Each year the Trust offers travelling fellowships in specific categories, one of which normally relates to a particular craft. Details are available in the summer of each year.

MAKING AN APPLICATION

Grant-giving bodies often ask you to complete an application form. This is likely to be their first contact with you so it helps if you try to make a good impression. If possible, type your entries; it looks more professional and is easier to read than handwriting. If you cannot type, always use black ink as it photocopies clearly and write legibly. This may seem petty, but when a committee has a hundred or more applications to go through it makes life much easier. If there is no application form, try and use headed notepaper as it looks more professional.

Always do a trial run on paper, or better still on a photocopy of the form; it saves making mistakes, and you can keep the copy for reference. Before returning the application, check that you have enclosed the supporting material asked for. There is usually a good reason why 35mm slides rather than photographs are wanted, for instance, and failure to send the correct visual evidence of work can cause delay in processing the application. When you submit slides, photographs, illustrations or any loose sheets of information, label each one with your name. (For slides, use self-adhesive labels because the ones you lick with your tongue always detach themselves and jam the slide projector.) Indicate which way up each slide should be shown and pack them carefully; if you send them loose in an ordinary envelope they are likely to arrive smashed. Always send a list describing your slides or photographs (materials used, size, date made, etc.). In most cases this will be asked for on the application form.

Good visual evidence of your work is *essential.* First-stage decisions are often made on the basis of slides or photographs, so weak pictures are worse than no pictures.

What else should accompany your application? A folder with any press clippings or other information may be useful. Your curriculum vitae should be up to date and, apart from giving your name, address and training, it should list exhibitions or publications in which you have appeared and mention any relevant work experience you have had. A short, unpretentious statement about your work will interest people, especially if it includes details about materials and any special methods used. Do try and send only what is relevant. Committee members will not welcome having to wade through masses of paper that has no direct bearing on the application. You will find that most organisations are unable to accept actual pieces of work at the first stages of selection because of the administrative problems involved.

Try and find out as much as you can about the organisation you are applying to and what they will be looking for. The Crafts Council, for instance, keeps copies of slides of Setting-Up Grant recipients' work. These can be consulted in the Information Section during opening hours. It may be useful to know who will be on the committee and most organisations will be happy to tell you this. Do not be afraid to ask any questions you may have about the particular scheme you are applying under, but check these are not already answered in the accompanying guidelines! If you have several queries, it may be worth making an appointment to talk with the administrator before actually completing the form.

Make sure that the application and attendant information arrive a few days before the deadline. Finally, try not to be too despondent if your application is rejected. Most selection processes are very competitive, with only a small number of applicants being successful.

BANKS

It is likely that at some point you will look to your bank to lend you some money. It is equally likely that you already have an overdraft and maybe also the accompanying letters of regret from your bank manager! The first point to make is that if your relationship with your bank is a bad one, then it is perhaps best to close that account and move to another bank. This can be particularly relevant if you are just leaving college, as inadequate student grants may have led to a stormy relationship. If you do open an account with another bank you will have a fresh start.

Whether you are starting your workshop business or developing it, you should try to borrow enough money to help you function through the first difficult months. You may decide to operate by having an overdraft or by getting a loan, but in either case you must arrange this with your bank manager in advance. There is no point in trying to operate on an overdraft only to have your cheques suddenly bounce because you did not get permission to increase your overdraft limit. If this happens, your business will be in trouble as suppliers will not accept your cheques or give you credit, therefore you must either arrange an overdraft limit (and stay within it) or arrange a loan. An overdraft is the most common form of funding for a small business, the advantage being that interest is calculated on the actual level of borrowing day to day (usually 2-3% over bank base rate). The disadvantage is that it is less secure than a loan and the interest rate will fluctuate in line with the bank rate.

A bank loan is normally only given for a specific purpose, such as buying equipement or renovating your workshop. The advantage of a loan is that you receive a specific sum of money and know in advance the regular repayments which must be made. Loans are normally given for one to five years and cost slightly more than an overdraft. It is quite possible to borrow in both ways; a loan for equipment and an overdraft for day-to-day running costs.

Approaching a bank manager can be unnerving, but remember that a bank's business is lending money so you should not feel embarrassed about asking. Try and present yourself in a professional way. Prepare your information and proposal in advance and send it to your bank manager with a letter requesting an appointment. Include a c.v. outlining your qualifications and experience, an outline proposal of what you plan to do, details of the type of work you plan to produce, a cash flow statement (see page 22) and the amount of loan required. If you have photos of your work or newspaper cuttings, send those – anything that will help emphasise your serious approach. When you go along for the appointment, make sure that you know exactly how much of a loan you require and what security you could offer. The simplest form of security is to have the loan guaranteed by someone whom the bank trusts to repay the loan, should you not. This can be a more business-like way of obtaining help from a relative or friend; you might be doubtful about asking them for cash straight out, but asking them to act a guarantor may be more acceptable. Also they will not actually have to put up any cash – unless your workshop fails. Other types of security include property, other funds such as a building society account, stocks and shares, etc. It can be useful to take along one or more pieces of work so that the manager will clearly see what you make and the quality of the making.

If you are successful in obtaining a loan or overdraft, ensure that you keep the bank informed. If you start running into financial difficulties, tell the bank in advance rather than waiting for them to find out. If you receive any publicity or have an exhibition, let your bank manager know.

If you are unsuccessful in obtaining assistance, it may be worth trying another bank.

There are a series of schemes designed to assist small businesses with borrowing, although these tend to be less relevant to very small businesses. However, it may be worth asking your bank about the government-backed Loan Guarantee Scheme or any similar scheme operated by the bank itself.

ADMINISTRATION

All too often self-employed businesses fail not because of their work but because of poor administration. This chapter is therefore designed to help you tackle the basic administrative tasks involved in running your business.

The first essential is to sort out your tax and National Insurance position. If you are running your own business, you are technically ineligible for Unemployment or Supplementary Benefit. However, certain local offices do allow some flexibility to people starting up in business; it may be worth your while to go along, explain that you are about to set up but will have no income for the initial period, and ask their advice about continuing to draw benefit. If you clarify your tax and NI position as soon as possible after you set up, you will avoid difficulties later on.

Similarly, if you organise book-keeping and paperwork systems early on you will make life easier; the longer you leave these jobs, the more complicated they become. People often shy away from book-keeping and other necessary paperwork because they seem so complex, but it is perfectly possible to set up simple systems which work well for most craft businesses (see page 20).

Administration cannot be avoided so the most realistic approach is to come to terms with it. You may never reach the stage where you enjoy book-keeping and other administrative tasks, but at least you can reduce the amount of worry and time expended on them by understanding what needs to be done, organising a system which suits you, and dealing with it on a regular basis.

THE LEGAL FRAMEWORK OF THE BUSINESS

Almost every craftsman or woman starts their business by "working for themselves", i.e. technically they become **sole traders.** A few team up with one or more like-minded individuals and without further formalities start work; they are **partners.** And there are a very few who from the beginning set up a **limited company** or a **co-operative.**

Sole trader This is the simplest form of business set-up requiring no legal formalities whatsoever, simply a private decision to start trading. For most new crafts businesses it is the obvious choice; the craftsperson is in complete control and takes all the profit (or loss!), there are no legal setting up costs and less annual paperwork. The tax position may also be slightly advantageous in the case of a young business. There is nothing to stop a sole trader from taking on employees.

The only real disadvantage of this form of trading is that if the business fails, creditors can take legal action not only against business assets for the money owed to them, but also against any private assets, for example your house. This is why businessmen and women sometimes transfer major assets into their spouse's name so that they will not be at risk. (They are, of course, running another risk in the event of a divorce.)

Although this form of business requires no legal formalities to commence, both the DHSS and the Inland Revenue must be informed and you will be required to pay National Insurance stamps week by week and income tax on the profits of the business.

If you decide to trade under any name other than your own (for example, as "Blackbird Pottery" rather than Anthony Potter or A. Potter), whilst you no longer have to register the business name, you must disclose the real name and address of the owner on all business paperwork including letters, orders, invoices and receipts. In addition you must display this information clearly in any business premises to which customers and suppliers have access. Full details of the requirements are available from the Small Firms Service.

Partnership A partnership is merely an extension of the set-up under the previous heading of "sole trader", but in this case two or more people are carrying on the business and sharing the profits (or losses) between them in usually equal portions. No legal formalities are required to set up a partnership and nothing need be stated in writing, but in practice it is of the utmost importance that a written partnership agreement is drawn up, preferably by a solicitor. Partnerships often last a long time and, as in marriages, over the years situations and attitudes change so that when the end comes bitter legal fights can develop over the property acquired. Have a partnership agreement prepared and signed, and then file it away. You will discover that when the time comes and you need to refer to it, that will be when the partnership is under strain.

Amongst other matters, the partnership agreement should cover the following points: the purpose of the partnership; the amount of capital to be put in by each partner; the role of each partner; the apportioning of profits; the duration of the partnership; the arrangements for dissolving the partnership, including the retirement or death of a partner; how the bank account is to be operated; the hours of work and holidays allotted; provision in the event of a long sickness of one partner; and arrangements for arbitration disagreement.

The advantage of a partnership is that two or more people working together are more cost-effective and bring to the business a range of complementary skills. There is also the question of moral support; difficult decisions may be easier to take after joint discussions. Like the sole trader, a business run as a partnership is cheap to set up, with no legal formalities, and it can employ others. The requirements to inform the DHSS and the Inland Revenue and to disclose the names of the proprietors are exactly the same.

The disadvantages are the same as for the sole trader but with one further point; each partner is responsible for the business debts and errors of the other(s). Thus, if the business fails and one partner does not pay his share of the debts, the other partner(s) will be required to pay not only their own share but also the share of the first partner. This even extends to tax debts. In a partnership you assume responsibility for all debts incurred by the business even if they were incurred by another partner's dishonesty or mismanagement without your knowledge, so think very carefully before entering into a partnership. For a small crafts business the advantages of having someone to talk to or of sharing machinery may be gained merely by sharing a workshop. You do not have to be partners.

Finally, a husband and wife can enter into a business partnership but it is often more advantageous for tax reasons for one (usually the wife) to be an employee.

Limited company Some businesses are set up from the start as limited companies; other small businesses run, for example, by a "sole trader" decide to turn themselves into a limited company as the business grows. Either way, the main advantage is that, because the limited company has its independent legal identity, the sole trader who has now become the director of the company is liable for no more than the nominal value of the share held in the company. In other words, his/her personal possessions are not at risk. Another possible advantage is that suppliers sometimes treat a company, albeit small, with greater respect than they do a sole trader.

However, the advantages are not especially great, for a bank manager lending money to a small limited company, or a landlord granting a lease to one, will usually insist that the director gives a personal guarantee. Thus the advantage of the limited liability is largely eroded. Furthermore, it is quite expensive to set up a company, record-keeping is likely to be more extensive and accountants' fees therefore higher. Clearly, before setting up a limited company it will be worth discussing all the pros and cons with your accountant, bank manager and solicitor.

Co-operative Craftspeople who are intending to work in some joint situation, perhaps by sharing a workshop, are sometimes tempted to think that by setting up a co-operative the problems of joint decision-making will be solved. They will not and craftspeople who, by definition, are producing and selling individual work will almost certainly find that the co-operative structure will not allow them sufficient control over their own businesses.

TAXATION

Everyone who receives an income is liable to pay tax on it. Rates of tax are set at a percentage of your taxable income, which is everything you earn or receive from investments less your personal allowance (a fixed amount which varies depending whether you are married or single) and allowances for such things as mortgage interest, dependant relatives, etc. As soon as you start your own business or workshop, you should advise your local Inspector of Taxes by completing and sending in a Form 41G. This form and full information about tax is contained in the Inland Revenue's booklet "Starting in Business", available free from your local tax office.

While it is not impossible for the self-employed to deal directly with their local tax office, most people find it difficult and it is far better to employ an accountant. Your accountant will prepare your annual accounts, taking into consideration all allowable business expenditure, and will negotiate the tax assessment on your behalf with the tax office. It is a good idea to employ an accountant immediately you start your business as he/she will be able to advise on book-keeping and give you some idea of your likely tax liability, if any.

If you are established as a sole trader or part of a partnership, you are liable for income tax under Schedule D; if you are incorporated as a limited company, you pay corporation tax. Under Schedule D tax is payable on your profit, which is the balance of your income left after deducting all expenses incurred wholly and exclusively for the purposes of your business. Your income includes fees and grants, for example a Setting Up or Enterprise Allowance Scheme grant. The main part of your income will come from sales and commissions.

Expenses normally include workshop overheads (rent, rates, light, heat, telephone, travel, postage, motor vehicle expenses, bank charges, interest on loans, bad debts, accountancy and legal fees, etc.), materials and wages (apart from your own). Where certain items, such as your car or telephone, are used for both business and personal purposes, an appropriate proportion of the total sum should be claimed. If you are working from home a proportion of the household expenses may also be claimed, but if you own your house be careful as any profit from selling the property may be partially assessed for capital gains tax. Check this point with your accountant. Capital expenditures such as the purchase of equipment or a motor vehicle qualify for special allowances; again ask your accountant's advice.

Once your profit has been computed, your annual accounts are submitted to the Inland Revenue along with a tax return. Provided the Tax Inspector agrees the accounts, an assessment will be issued. The assessment is made on a "preceding year" basis, which means that the tax you are due to pay in one year will be based on the profit made in the previous year. Thus you are paying tax retrospectively and if your profits are such that you will be due to pay tax you should put funds aside for this purpose.

If a loss is made in any one year, this can either be offset against other income (for example, from part-time work) or carried forward and set against future profits. If you are married, your loss can be offset against the income of your spouse. However, if losses occur regularly over a number of years the Tax Inspector may disallow further claims for relief, on the grounds that you are not running a proper business but merely engaged in a hobby.

CHOOSING AN ACCOUNTANT

The best way to find an accountant is to ask for recommendations from friends who are already working in business on their own. If that is not possible, your bank manager may be able to offer advice. Try to find an accountant who is used to dealing with self-employed people, ideally some of whom are craftspeople, and someone you like.

Accountants can provide useful advice on book-keeping, etc. but remember that advice will cost money. Many accountants will be reluctant to quote their likely annual charge, given that they will not know how much advice you require or the state of your books, but it is worth asking for a rough idea. It is worth shopping around as accountants' fees can vary enormously, although you have to equate the cost with the service each provides. If you feel dissatisfied with the service or the cost, the best thing is to tell the accountant so. This may seem obvious but it is all too easy not to say anything, and often talking about a problem can quickly lead to its solution. If you continue to be dissatisfied then you should not hesitate to change to someone else.

NATIONAL INSURANCE

If you are self-employed for all or part of the time, you must arrange to make National Insurance contributions unless your earnings in a year are less than £2,350 (1989-90 lower limit). As a self-employed person you must pay flat-rate Class 2 contributions and also Class 4 contributions.

Class 2 contributions must be paid every week including holidays at the rate of £4.25 a week. You can make payments either by stamping a contribution card (obtainable from your local Social Security office) with National Insurance stamps which can be bought from the Post Office, or by arranging for contributions to be automatically paid from your bank or Giro account by direct debit. To arrange this you complete Form CF351 which is attached to the booklet "National Insurance Guide for the Self-Employed", Ref. N141. It is simpler to arrange to pay by direct debit rather than buying stamps as you will not be in danger of forgetting to buy stamps or of losing the card, which can mean having to pay the contributions again.

Class 4 contributions are paid on top of Class 2 contributions and are assessed and collected by the Inland Revenue. The assessment will be based on your profits for the year and the 1989-90 figure was 6.3% of the amount of profits exceeding £5,050. Payment of Class 4 contributions is made as part of payment of your tax, which in the case of self-employed people is in half-yearly instalments. 50% of Class 4 contributions are tax-deductable.

Exemption from contributions can be applied for if your profits in the year are, or are expected to be, less than £2,350 (1989-90 figure); if this is the case use Form CF10 which is included in the leaflet "People with Small Earnings from Self-Employment", Ref. NI 27a. *Exemption must be applied for* – you cannot just not pay contributions because your earnings fall below the limit. Do not leave your application too late.

If you are employed elsewhere for part of the time you will have to pay Class 1 contributions as well and these contributions will automatically be deducted by your employer. However, there is an upper level to the amount of contributions you have to pay in any tax year and if your total contributions are more than this the excess will be refunded to you. In certain circumstances, to avoid the need for a refund you can ask to postpone payment of Class 2 and Class 4 contributions until your exact liability is known – an option worth investigating if you are earning quite a bit from part-time work.

If you have employees see pages 117–122

The Department of Health and Social Security issues a number of leaflets which explain these points in detail. The relevant ones are:
"National Insurance Guide for the Self-Employed" (Form N141)
"Class 4 NI Contributions" (Form NP18)
"Social Security Benefit Rates" (Form NI 196)
"National Insurance Contribution Rates" (Form NI 208)
"People with Small Earnings from Self-Employment" (Form NI 27a)
"More than One Job? Class 1 Contributions" (Form NP28)
"NI Contributions for Employees" (Form NI 40)
These are all available free from your local DHSS office.

It is important to make sure that you do start paying National Insurance contributions when you start your own business or workshop, unless you have been exempted; failure to do so can lead to prosecution and will certainly involve you in having to pay all the amount due in arrears if it is discovered that you have been operating as self-employed but not paying NI contributions.

PENSIONS

Your National Insurance payments ensure that you will receive the basic State pension on reaching retirement age, but as this is generally considered to be inadequate you may wish to consider investing in additional pension rights, especially as there are substantial tax benefits involved. If so, consult your accountant or insurance broker for details of the various possible schemes.

BASIC BOOK-KEEPING

There are several different systems of book-keeping:

The "shoe-box" system

This is the simplest system. You need five filing (or shoe) boxes, a bank paying-in book, a cheque book and a notebook.

Keep two of the filing boxes for unpaid invoices (one for sales and one for purchases, services, etc.). The other two boxes are for paid invoices (again, one for sales and one for purchases, services, etc.). When you receive payment for a sales invoice, mark on your copy the date payment was received and transfer it to the box for paid sales invoices. Similarly, when you pay an invoice for purchases, services, etc., put on it the date you paid it and transfer it to the paid purchase invoice box. By adding together all the invoices in the unpaid invoice box (sales) you can find out how much you are owed, and by adding together all the invoices in the other unpaid invoices box (purchases) how much you owe. Pay all cash and cheques received into the bank, recording the amounts in your paying-in book. All cheques should be recorded on your cheque book stubs. By adding on pay-ins and deducting cheques issued, you can keep a running account of your bank balance. The notebook is merely to record all small day-to-day cash expenditure relating to the business, as a tax record (bus fares, parking, stationery, etc.). In addition you should keep all cash receipts, etc. relating to the business in the fifth box.

This system is perfectly adequate if your turnover is small, and should enable your accountant to draw up annual accounts. However, there are disadvantages. It does not allow you any cash control and it is weak on credit control. Credit control is basically watching that payments due to you do not take too long to be paid. One answer is to go through the box relating to unpaid invoices (sales) at regular intervals and make sure none have been outstanding for too long. Unless you have agreed a longer payment period, it is worth sending out a statement after one month showing the amount outstanding as a reminder.

Bought systems

There are several book-keeping systems which can be purchased. These come with full instructions and examples for each section, which will be laid out ready for entries. The advantage of these is that they provide some measure of financial control, especially over cash and bank balances and credit control, and all incorporate the accounting of VAT. They aim to reduce the amount of work your accountant will have to do and so save you money on fees.

However, they all suffer from the same disadvantage, which is that none of them work unless they are kept up to date regularly, at least weekly and preferably daily. As a drawback this cannot be over-emphasised, for if they are allowed to get out of control it can cost even more in accountant's fees to sort them out! Also the instructions are often quite difficult for those who are not very good at figures to follow.

Clearly the system you choose will depend on the number of items you are selling, the number of customers, your turnover, whether or not you are registered for VAT, etc. Of the systems which can be purchased, here are three:

Simplex "D" Cash Book (available from W.H. Smith, price about £5). This is a hardback book with one record page for each week of the year, plus analysis pages. The book incorporates one year's accounts.

Finco Small Business Book-Keeping System (price about £50). Contains two years' supply of record sheets and gives a good amount of financial control.

Kalamazoo Set-Up (price about £100). Although more expensive, this is extremely comprehensive and in addition saves time by being a single write system (for example, entering up to three records simultaneously).

Cash flow statement

A cash flow is simply an estimate of how much you think you will earn and how much you think you will need to spend over a future period. Thus it is a projection of the flow of cash coming into and going out of the business. Remember that cheques count as cash. Cash flow statements assist you in looking ahead to your future financial position and therefore letting you see how much borrowing, if any, you will require. When you come to apply to a bank for a loan or overdraft, a cash flow statement will be necessary to enable the bank to see the level of borrowing required and your ability to repay.

Projections are normally tabled month by month as detailed in the example below. The monthly projections which you have made should be checked regularly against the actual monthly figures so that you can see whether the true position is as estimated, or whether it is worse or better.

Remember that invoices for sales will not normally be paid for a time, so when you are estimating the income from any sales billed by invoice you should presume that at least two months will elapse before the actual cash is received. For a cash flow statement it is advisable to show the worst situation. A typical cash flow statement for a small workshop would look like this:

CASH FLOW STATEMENT

	(note)	Jan £	Feb £	Mar £	Apr £	May £	Jun £	Jul £	Aug £	Sep £	Oct £	Nov £	Dec £	Total £
Receipts														
Cash sales	(1)	–	–	1200	800	700	400	800	700	1200	1350	1000	2100	10250
Teaching/other employment	(2)	–	–	–	150	–	–	–	–	180	–	–	–	330
Cash in	(3)	–	–	1200	950	700	400	800	700	1380	1350	1000	2100	10580
Payments	(4)													
Rent & rates		250	–	–	360	–	–	250	–	–	360	–	–	1220
Electricity/gas		150	–	–	175	–	–	75	–	–	100	–	–	500
Repairs/cleaning		40	–	–	–	50	–	10	–	40	–	–	–	140
Motor expenses		80	60	80	180	60	40	50	30	40	100	60	70	850
Telephone/postage		60	10	10	40	10	–	40	10	–	40	20	–	240
Photography/advertising		60	–	–	40	–	–	–	–	–	–	–	–	100
Craft fair fees		–	–	–	–	–	–	40	40	–	–	–	–	80
Accountant/insurance		–	–	–	80	–	70	–	–	–	–	–	–	150
Loan interest/payments	(5)													
Equipment	(6)	600	–	–	–	–	–	–	–	–	–	–	–	600
Sub total		1240	70	90	875	120	110	465	80	80	600	80	70	3880
Materials	(7)	650	–	300	–	–	300	–	–	600	–	–	–	1850
Cash drawings	(8)	300	300	300	300	300	300	300	300	300	300	300	300	3600
Cash out	(9)	2190	370	690	1175	420	710	765	380	980	900	380	370	9330
Net loss –/net profit +	(10)	–2190	–370	+510	–225	+280	–310	+35	+320	+400	+450	+620	+1730	
Cumulative total at end of each month	(11)	–2190	–2560	–2050	–2275	–1995	–2305	–2270	–1950	–1550	–1100	–480	+1250	

Notes

1. All the cash you estimate to receive each month from sales of work or designs.
2. For a one-person business it may be advisable to include fees from teaching or other employment which you expect to earn. This can help prove your ability to repay the hoped-for loan.
3. The total cash which you estimate to receive in each month.
4. A list of the payments you estimate to have to pay out under each heading per month.
5. Notice that no amounts are included here. However, were a loan to be forthcoming, repayment amounts would have to be included and the cash flow adjusted accordingly. When you are preparing your own cash flow, leave this line blank (unless you already have other loan repayments) and when you meet with your bank manager ask his/her advice on what monthly amount should go in. Thus you will have to borrow enough to take account of the repayments over the period.
6. Part of the reason for needing to borrow money may be to buy necessary equipment, so include any payments for this at the beginning of the period.
7. The cost of materials you expect to have to buy. As buying in bulk is often cheaper, it may be worth estimating most of your material purchases at the start of the period.
8. As you will need some cash to exist on, you will make cash drawings each week or month. In a self-employed business cash drawings are the equivalent to wages to yourself.
9. The total cash which you estimate to pay out each month.
10. The loss or profit in each month. Thus, in February there will be no income and bills/drawings will total £370, hence a net loss for that month of £370. In August you estimate to receive £700 and pay out £380, thus giving a net profit of £320 in that month.
11. The cumulative total which results from adding on the next month's result. If your bank acccount were starting at zero, then this would be the estimate of your bank balance at the end of each month. It estimates that your highest borrowing need will be in February and that by December you will be in credit.

This is the guide your bank manager (and you) require to be able to judge what level of loan or overdraft you will need, and to estimate how long it will be before it can be repaid or cleared.

PAPERWORK

Stationers sell pads of invoices and delivery notes to which you can add your name and address, but it is better to have something which looks more professional and reflects the quality of the work you are selling. The simplest answer is to have a letterhead printed, stating who you are, your address and what you do. A business card with the same information is also useful.

Printing is relatively cheap, but the preparation of the original artwork is expensive so it is worth doing it yourself or finding a friendly graphic artist to do it for you – maybe you can pay them with a piece of your work. If you do it yourself, use Letraset on white paper (A4 size is best); this will produce an adequate copy for an "instant printer" to use. Local print shops produce letterheads reasonably inexpensively, but make sure that the quality is good.

Using your letterheaded notepaper as a basis, you need six documents for your trading:

Order form for purchasing goods or raw materials. It should state the date, the quantity, description of goods, price and delivery details (where applicable).

Delivery note This accompanies goods, whether despatched or delivered. It should state the customer's name and order number, the quantity, price and description of goods delivered. If you deliver yourself, always get a signature on your copy as confirmation of receipt.

Sale-or-return record for recording work left on sale or return. It should be dated and should state the retailer's name and the quantity, description and price of each item. Makes sure that the retailer signs your copy.

Invoice This is a request for payment and should be sent separately from the goods when you are supplying a firm, although with private clients it can be handed over with the goods. It carries the same information as the delivery note or sale-or-return record (an "invoice" for goods left on sale or return is sent when these have subsequently been sold) plus the number of that document, the total cost, any discounts, VAT and VAT number where applicable.

Credit note If goods are returned for any reason, make sure that you keep a record, otherwise there may be a dispute at a later stage as to whether you delivered the goods or not. When the returned goods are received, send the customer a credit note stating the order number, quantity, the type and price of each item, and the reason for return. If

and when the goods are replaced, send a fresh invoice.
Statement This is a reminder to the customer that he/she has not yet paid. It quotes any unpaid invoices, totals them and deducts any credit notes issued.

In every case, be sure to take a carbon copy and file it. Include the date (the day posted) and number each category consecutively to help in your book-keeping and to guard against loss. Do not start numbering at 1 as this has an amateur look. Start at 100 or 200 to make it appear that you have been trading for some time.

ACCOUNTING FOR VALUE ADDED TAX (VAT)

If your annual turnover (not your profit or personal income) exceeds, or is likely to exceed, the declared level (£23,600 in 1989) then you are legally required to register with your local VAT office of the Customs and Excise. Note that you must also register if your turnover in any quarter is more than £8,000. It is possible to ask to be registered even if your turnover does not reach the declared level; this can be worth considering if your craft means that you use expensive materials which carry VAT or if you export most of what your produce. (Exports are zero-rated.) However, this is something to first discuss with your accountant.

When you register, you will be allocated a certificate showing your VAT number and this number must be included on all your invoices and statements. These records must all clearly show the rate of VAT (15%) and the total amount charged.

Example invoice

10 jugs @ £4.23	42.30
VAT @ 15%	6.35
	£48.65

VAT no. 2723647

Anything you purchase is called an "input"; on some purchases you will be charged VAT and on some you will not. Anything you sell is an "output" and if you are registered you must charge VAT on all sales. At regular intervals (normally quarterly) you will have to make a return of all your outputs, showing their total value and the amount of VAT charged. Against this you set the total of your inputs and the VAT paid. If the VAT on outputs exceeds the VAT on inputs, the difference will be payable to the Customs and Excise. If it is the other way round, then the Customs and Excise will reimburse you.

For more detailed information, consult "Should I Be Registered?" (No 700/1/88) (free from Customs and Excise).

If you are registered for VAT, you will be involved in quite a bit of extra adminstration as you will have to keep detailed records of your sales and purchases.

If you are registered and are considering buying an expensive piece of equipment or materials, it is worth arranging to be invoiced just before you are about to make your next VAT return. The VAT on the purchase will be offset even though you may not have actually paid the invoice.

When you sell a piece of work that has been held on a sale-or-return basis, you should include the total selling price (less any VAT) in your income and also record the shop's commission or mark-up as an expenditure. For example, if you leave an object (wholesale price £54) with a shop on a sale-or-return basis and they then sell it for £86.40 (£54 plus 60% mark-up), you would record £86.40 as sales income and £32.40 as commission in your expenditure accounts. This is the standard method of accounting for sales of sale-or-return work for VAT purposes; it is also a good way of showing a higher turnover, which can be useful if you are seeking a bank loan or mortgage.

BANK ACCOUNT

It is advisable to open a separate bank account for your business; it will help you to keep your books and help your accountant to finalise your annual accounts. To begin with, you may just decide to open a number two bank account as a way of avoiding the higher bank charges levied on business accounts, but if you are doing quite a lot of trading your bank is likely to notice and to raise the charge accordingly. It may therefore be best to see your bank manager, explain that you are setting up your own crafts workshop but are unlikely to earn much in the first year or two, and to ask him/her to consider waiving the normal business service charges for an agreed period. Some banks are offering free banking to people on the Government's Enterprise Allowance Scheme.

Reconciling your bank statement

You should arrange for bank statements to be sent to you monthly. When you receive each statement, check to see if there are any receipts or charges which you have not included in your records and, if so, enter these. If you are operating the "shoe-box" system, receipts should be recorded on a stub of your paying-in-book and added to the running bank balance in your cheque book; charges should be recorded on your cheque book stub and deducted from the running balance. If you are using a cash book, then receipts will go on the credit side (payments), charges on the debit side (receipts). The next step is to reconcile the balance shown in your cheque book or cash book with that shown on the statement:

		£
Date:	Credit balance as bank statement	
	Add amounts banked but not yet included in the bank statement	
	Deduct cheques issued but not yet included in the bank statement	
	Balance shown in your records	

If your bank account is overdrawn, amounts banked but not yet included are then deducted and cheques not yet included are added.

If the balance does not agree with your records, check your record of payments and cheques against the bank statement to see if there are any discrepancies or if you have missed something out.

INSURANCE

With all matters of insurance, it is best to consult a qualified insurance broker who will be able to advise you on your needs and the cost. Insurance brokers do not charge for their services; instead they receive commission from the insurance companies.

The National Enterprise Insurance Scheme has been set up to assist those starting businesses to find suitable business insurance. Contact Stafford Knight & Co Ltd, 4/5 London Wall Buildings, London EC2M 5NR.

The following types of insurance should be considered:

Public Liability If your workshop is visited by members of the public you should take out this insurance against any claims for injury or damage to third parties caused by your alleged negligence. It is also worth considering extending this to cover your goods, **Products Liability**, given that any article can be potentially dangerous.

Motor Insurance Check that your vehicle insurance covers your business activities.

Employers Liability If you employ others, you are legally required to take out this insurance.

Fire & Theft You should insure your workshop, equipment and stock. If you are working from home you must ensure that your home insurance is altered to include your workshop activity or you will be in danger of having any claims refused.

Goods in Transit Worth considering to cover work being transported.

Personal Accident If you are injured or become ill you may have to give up work for a time which would result in loss of income.

TELEPHONE

Telephone calls made in the morning are more expensive than those in the afternoon so try and limit outgoing calls to the afternoon (or, better still, the evening). Also try and keep calls short. It is important that people can contact you by telephone and an answering machine will ensure that people can at least leave a message. Prospective customers are likely to fade away if after two or three attempts to phone you they do not get through. Another advantage of an answering machine is that it cuts down interruptions while you are working. The disadvantages of answering machines are that some people dislike leaving messages on them and that you can end up paying more in outgoing calls phoning back. However, on balance they are a valuable help to any small business where it is not feasible to have someone available to answer the phone all the time.

ORGANISING YOUR TIME

Organising your time can be difficult given the range of tasks to be done and the sudden demands and crises which require urgent attention. But it is essential that you exercise some control or you will find yourself rushing from one thing to another in a fragmented way. If you keep a check on your use of time, you can watch out for the natural inclination to put off doing things which you do not want to do. Planning your work is more efficient as it helps you to concentrate on work for specific blocks of time.

If you are working under pressure there is a tendency to respond to each new demand instantly, when in fact this is often unnecessary. Placing tasks in order of priority will help you to counteract this and assist you in keeping to essential deadlines.

Given that the cost of your work is related to the hours spent making, the first priority is to ensure that your making time does not fall below a set number of hours each working week. The second priority is selling your work and promoting yourself, and again you should allocate a specified amount of time per week or month as a minimum.

It can be helpful to keep a strict record of how your time is spent for a week or two, as an experiment. Such a record will show the actual situation, which may be quite different from what you believe to be the case. You will be able to see the percentage of time spent on making (useful in costing your work), administration, selling, etc., and if the balance is wrong consider how best to adjust your pattern of working.

Although it is important that you do not waste working time, you should not get too worried about the odd hour spent chatting to the maker next door or sketching the view out of the window. You are your own boss and if you have worked twelve hours the day before, then a couple of hours off the next day may be just the break you need to keep you happy. There is little point in being a craftsperson and working long hours for little cash if you do not get satisfaction from the life. It is difficult to retain integrity about your work if you stop enjoying yourself.

One way to help ease your time problems is to employ people to do the things you are not good at. A book-keeper may do in a couple of hours what would take you days to finish, and the extra making time thus released may make it worthwhile to employ someone for a few hours a week. Similary, part-time help for simple labouring tasks may be cost-effective in terms of your time saved. Colleges are often keen to place students temporarily for work experience and, although this can often waste as much time as it saves in telling them what to do, some students are extremely useful.

Another way to ease time problems is to pool tasks with other makers. It may be that there are three makers in your area, all of whom are regularly visiting the same outlets to deliver work and collect materials, and some form of "pool" system could save everyone time and money. Such co-operation could extend to attending craft fairs where a stand could be jointly hired, or to joint publicity, meaning that everyone's limited resources would stretch further. Guilds and societies are well placed to initiate such co-operation and many already do, so check to see if this is another good reason for joining the one relevant to your work.

FINDING A SOLICITOR

Most small businesses will need a solicitor sooner or later, but, unlike an accountant who will hopefully keep a watchful eye on the business month by month, a solicitor is generally employed for a specific purpose. Services do not come cheaply but for certain purposes it is foolish not to use them; the results of DIY legal drafting can be very expensive indeed if a legal battle arises. The most obvious areas for caution are buying or leasing property, forming a partnership or limited company, or making a will. However, solicitors are often a mine of information and advice and it is as well to make contact with a suitable firm fairly early on in the life of your business. A detailed reference book on the laws relating to small business is *Croner's Reference Book for the Self-Employed and Smaller Business.* The book is updated monthly on a loose-leaf system and is obtainable from Croner House, 173 Kingston Road, New Malden, Surrey KT3 3SS.

As with accountants, the best way to find a good solicitor is by personal recommendation. However, most solicitors specialise to some extent and you should not assume that the solicitor who dealt with the transfer of your friend's house will necessarily be prepared to act for you in taking action against a gallery which refuses to pay. Even if they are prepared to act, they may not be as efficient as a firm which specialises in this area of work. An alternative source of recommendation is to write to The Law Society, 113 Chancery Lane, London WC2 and ask for a list of solicitors in your county; this list sets out the specialities of each practice and grades them A, B or C according to the volume of work they handle in each area. They also run a scheme "Lawyers for Enterprise" which offers a free consultation on legal matters. The first session will indicate the help that can be given and estimate the cost.

Generally speaking, smaller crafts business should avoid the very large firms where the fees may be higher and the partners too busy to consider your affairs. Instead go for the small to medium sized firm in the nearest large town, where you can build up a personal relationship over the years.

Making a will

As a postscript to this chapter is is appropriate to remind you to make a will, especially if you have dependants or assets. Admittedly, making a will will not make running your workshop and business any easier, but it may bring a little peace of mind in the knowledge that if you die the legal process of sorting out your business affairs and assets will be more straightforward, and probably more beneficial, for those you leave behind. A solicitor will not charge much more to draw up a will than the cost of a modest meal for two, and the effect lasts rather longer.

PREMISES

Choosing a workspace will depend on a variety of factors – your personal preferences, what you can afford, the types of workshop available, etc. – and you will probably have to settle for a space that does not meet all your requirements. Before even beginning to look for a workshop, make a checklist of your requirements and put them in order of importance. Then if you find a workshop that meets, say the top five, you will decide to take it. Be careful not to end up in a workshop that is too small or too depressing. You will probably spend more time in your workshop than at home, so it is important to have a space that is relatively pleasant to be in; if the space is too restricted or grim, your work is likely to suffer.

WORKING FROM HOME

Technically anyone operating a business from their home needs to have planning permission. To obtain planning permission, contact the planning department of your local council and tell them what you propose; they will inform you if there are any restrictions and how these can be met. Planning authorities have been instructed to assist small businesses in setting up and you should find them helpful, especially if you ask their advice in good time rather than after you have started. Having said this, a great number of small businesses, including craft workshops, are conducted from home without council permission. This is a dangerous and illegal procedure, and if you attract the council's attention (by causing noise, black smoke or whatever) you may be ordered to stop operating.

Provided you are not causing a public nuisance, it is permissible to make crafts at a hobby level. What this means is a matter of opinion, so if you decide to operate without planning permission do at least ensure that you keep on good terms with your neighbours and generally avoid drawing attention to yourself. However, do check with your local council if you plan to employ other people in the workshop, make alterations to the building, use noisy machinery or dangerous chemicals, or have lots of people coming to buy work.

You should also take account of your tenancy agreement, lease or mortgage. Where would you stand with your insurance company or building society, for example, if there was a fire resulting from your business activities? By working from home you may be breaking the terms of such agreements, which could lead to their termination if you have not obtained permission. Insurance policies are issued on the basis of your providing all relevant information, so if you work from home without informing the insurance company you could be in danger of nullifying your policy. If you are not increasing the risks (by using volatile chemicals, machinery, etc.), informing them should not materially affect the premium you have to pay.

RENTING A WORKSHOP

If you decide to rent a space outside the home, there are two alternatives: to rent space in a group workshop, or in an individual workshop.

Group workshops

The Crafts Council has a list of group workshops throughout the country, available free on request. There are two main types of group workshop. One involves the workshop being open to the public, either for all or part of the time. Some of these offer rents which are less than the normal going commercial rental. All normally offer the opportunity for selling direct to the public. Whether or not such a situation appeals to you will tend to depend on your ability to work in front of the public. You should take account of the fact that interruptions will tend to reduce the amount of time available for making. Also you will need to consider if the people visiting the centre are likely to want to buy your work.

Other group workshops are developments where a building contains a number of units, not open to the public. These are particularly popular as they combine the advantages of your own workshop with some contact with people working in similar disciplines. Working on your own can be difficult, especially when things are not going well, and a group workshop offers the chance to exchange ideas and share problems. Some group workshops offer central services such a secretarial help, book-keeping and a selling/ gallery space. Such assistance can be of great help and it can also make things easier for buyers as they can visit several makers at one time.

The group can combine to organise various promotional activities, for instance, 401½ Workshops in London have held exhibitions of past and present members' work, and Kingsgate Workshops now hold an annual event where the studio workshops are open to the public for about a week once a year. This is a particularly good way of encouraging new buyers and journalists to see your work.

Both types of group workshop may not be exclusively for crafts but may also include other small business.

Individual workshops

By far the best way of finding a workshop is by word of mouth, so let as many people as possible know you are looking. Advertisements are another good source of information – local newsagents, *Crafts* magazine and *Artists' Newsletter* always have details of space available. Your local council may be able to help you and some have lists of property for rent, but you should be prepared to wait a few weeks as the wheels tend to grind slowly in council departments.

Some craftspeople have found good workshops by looking for an empty building that would be suitable, discovering who is responsible for it and offering to make it usable for workshop space for, say, a rent-free period. Again, this sort of approach will take time. It may be worth combining with others looking for space and finding somewhere to rent jointly. Some areas of the country offer special assistance to those needing small workshops and it is worth consulting your local council's small business division for information. The Rural Development Commission also produces a list of workshops it has available.

Points to consider

Whatever type of space you decide to rent, the following points should be considered:

What part of the country should you choose? Should it be an urban or a rural area? You will need to think about your market; if you have to travel miles to deliver work, this could prove costly. Alternatively, if you are hoping people will come to you, you must be sure you are accessible – a mile down a bumpy track may deter potential customers! Think about your neighbours; if you are selling direct to the public, will a constant stream of customers (at least in the summer) cause a problem? For some crafts (saltglazed ceramics, for instance) there is no choice but to be in the country because of pollution problems.

How much can you afford? Find out whether the rent you have been quoted includes rates, and if not find out how much they are (in London they can often work out more expensive than the rent). Rents are often expressed in cost per square foot per year, for example, studio size 20 × 16 ft @ £4 per sq ft will cost £1280 per annum, or about £25 per week.

Does the rent include heating and lighting, and any other services, such as secretarial help? If it does and this is fixed, do you really need these other services? (How often will you use a telex machine?) Try and find out how much all your overheads are likely to be. Can you really afford to run a workshop or should you perhaps think about working from home to begin with?

Is the space the right size? You do not want to be paying for space you are not using. On the other hand, you may want to allow for some expansion or additional equipment in the future.

What else is essential for the sort of work you do? For instance, do you need a good source of natural light? If you are using heavy machines, you must ensure that the floors are strong enough to take their weight, and if you use a loom a high ceiling may be required. If you need to bring in a large item of machinery, will you be able to get it through a door or window?

What sort of electricity supply does the workshop have? Some equipment requires three-phase, which is expensive to instal and in some places not available. Do you need gas? Is water available? A telephone is essential for running any sort of business; if one is not already installed, it is costly to have this done and often there is a long waiting list. How will you heat the workshop? Are there any restrictions about using portable gas or paraffin heaters, which can be dangerous?

Are there any restrictions on the use of certain types of equipment or materials? Are the fire precautions in the workshop adequate? Think about the potential hazards – the use of chemicals or spraying equipment. Is this likely to cause any problems, for you or your neighbours? Is there good ventilation? This is particularly important if you will be creating dust or fumes.

What restrictions are there on access? Can you use the workshop only at certain hours, and what about weekends? If you have a rush job to do, this could be vital. Are there any conditions linked to the space, such as having to open to the public at certain times? Is the workshop secure?

Think about relationships with the landlord and other tenants. Will you have to sign a lease or licence? (A lease gives you more security of tenure but many workshops are now offered by licence agreement.) If so, it is worth considering the length of the lease. For those starting up their first workshop a short, renewable lease is probably best. Discover who is responsible for maintenance and repairs. Usually the landlord will deal with anything external or communal, and you will be responsible for internal repairs to your own space. Make sure you have some form of written agreement. If you are sharing a workshop with others, make sure you are clear about what the arrangements are concerning ownership of and sale of equipment, use of joint facilities such as the telephone, and payment of bills. Again, it is best to have something in writing. You may think you are good friends but it is amazing how quickly you can fall out.

Once you decide on premises, it may be useful to make a list of the things which need doing before you can start production and the dates by which these should be completed. For example:

Week One
Move in. Instal three-phase electricity. Repair roof. Build shelves. Arrange connection of telephone.
Week Two
Decorate. Have equipment delivered and connected. Fix toilet. Have electricity checked.

Week Three
Have materials delivered. Organise work spaces.
Week Four
Start production.

EQUIPMENT

List the essential equipment you must have to start making. While it may be possible to get under way without everything you need, by borrowing equipment or using facilities elsewhere, you must be careful that such a situation will not lead to problems in fulfilling orders. For example, firing your work in someone else's kiln or at your old college can serve to test out the market but is unlikely to be satisfactory in the long term. Obtaining the essential equipment before you start is almost certainly going to make your business more efficient and will reduce problems.

Research the different types of equipment and the availability of good second-hand equipment. It is worth asking others working at your craft for their recommendations or criticisms. Also think hard about the size or power – easy to believe you are saving by buying a cheaper version, only to discover after a short while that it is too small or under-powered. When buying equipment, you must imagine your developing needs over a number of years and balance that against your available funds and the likely space you will have in your workshop. Be careful of getting equipment which is much larger than you really need or borrowing a lot of money to buy equipment that is not essential. For example, too large a kiln can hold up production, limit experimentation and cause major financial problems if a kiln load goes wrong. Equally, over-committing yourself financially to buy non-essential equipment can force you into doing work you would rather not do just to repay the loan.

LEGAL POINTS

Landlord and tenant law, leases and tenancy agreements You will need to instruct a solicitor to act for you in settling the exact terms of a lease or tenancy agreement, but it is as well if you can sort out the major terms at an early stage in the negotiations.

First what is the length of the lease and the rent, and can the rent be raised ("reviewed") during the term? If the lease is for more than three years, almost certainly the landlord will retain the right to raise the rent in line with market values.

Next, you should check who is responsible for repairing the premises. The normal arrangement on a shortish lease is for the landlord to agree to carry out external repairs, including structural work, the roof and drains, while the tenant becomes responsible for internal repairs, including the glass in the windows. On a short lease you might be responsible for internal decorations only, while on a long lease you may have to undertake all repairs. The exact wording of the repair clause can be crucial and your solicitor will advise.

Thirdly, if you want to share your premises or split it up amongst a number of people, will the landlord allow you to sub-let part of the premises?

Finally, if you wish to leave the workshop before the end of the lease, will you be allowed to transfer the remainder of it to someone else? If not, you may find yourself paying for premises you no longer want.

Planning permission, bye-law approval, fire regulations For the purposes of the planning regulations, crafts are classed as "light industry" and you should check with the local authority that the workshop you propose to rent has the necessary planning permission. If it does not, you will have to apply for permission. This can be a long, drawn-out process but it is usually possible to obtain an informal opinion fairly quickly as to the likely outcome of an application from the planning officer at the local authority.

If you intend to alter the building, again you may need planning permission, but almost certainly you will also have to comply with Building Regulations as well.

Finally, and especially if you intend to employ others, the premises must comply with fire regulations. More potential workshops have never got off the ground for this single reason than for any other.

Community Charge (Poll Tax) Those working from home may be liable to pay business rates on that part of the property used for business, as well as their individual charge.

COSTING

Costing enables you to calculate exactly what each object costs to make, so that you know what to charge when selling it. Knowing what your work should sell for is essential to the success of your workshop business, for if you are to survive you must cover the costs of the workshop and earn enough to live on.

Costing is basically straightforward but there are a number of approaches and in larger businesses costing can become very complex. However, for anyone running a small craft workshop it is best to have a simple method and this guide sets out one approach which you can then modify or expand to suit your own needs.

This costing method is designed for those working full time on their own at their craft. If you work part time at your craft and have other employment, calculate your costings as though you were working in the workshop full time and charge accordingly. If you share the workshop, then of course some of your overheads will be shared and you should adjust the annual cost accordingly.

To calculate what your work costs, you need to consider four ingredients: overheads, labour, materials and contingency/profit.

OVERHEADS

These are all the cost of running your workshop and business, which have to be paid whether or not you are making work. Overheads can be divided into four headings:

1. **Workshop expenses** include bills directly connected with running the workshop, such as rent or mortgage repayment, electricity, gas, cleaning, maintenance and repairs, etc. If you are working in your house, include a relevant percentage of the bills.

2. **Business expenses** include those bills which, although not directly linked to the workshop, are essential parts of running your business, such as telephone, postage, travelling/motor car expenses, photography, advertising, craft fair fees, insurance, accountant's fee etc.

3. **Equipment/loans** If you have bought equipment, an amount to cover the replacement cost should be included – this is called depreciation. Reflect the expected life of the equipment by dividing the cost by the number of years which you expect the equipment to last, for example, £1,000 equipment expected to last five years should be charged at £200 each year (£1,000 ÷ 5). The reason for making this depreciation charge is that you will hopefully make a profit and have cash in the bank when the time comes to replace the equipment. As regards loans connected with the business (for equipment or starting-up capital), the cost of the annual repayments and interest charges must also be included.

4. **Stock** If you keep stocks of raw materials these will cost you money just sitting on the shelf as you will have to pay for them initially,

probably by borrowing money. If the stock is precious metal or expensive components, this can amount to a lot of money. To cover this, at least 20% of the average stock value should be added to the overheads, in addition to any loan/overdraft costs. Even if the amount is small, include it as a reminder to keep your material stocks as low as possible.

To work out the first element of your costing, you need to estimate what your annual overheads will be or have been in previous years. Clearly, with so many different things to take into account, everyone's overheads will be very different and the example below is merely to provide a working model.

Example: annual overheads of a small workshop	£
Rent	1,000
Rates	220
Gas and electricity	500
Maintenance and repairs	120
Cleaning materials	20
Telephone	160
Motor expenses, parking, etc.	850
Postage and stationery	80
Photography and advertising	100
Craft fair fees	80
Accountant	70
Insurance	80
Loan interest/repayments	360
Stock (20% of £400)	80
Equipment (£600 over 5 years)	120
Total	£3,840

Thus, in our example it costs £3,840 to run the workshop over a year. The next step is to calculate this annual cost as an hourly rate. First divide by the number of weeks worked in the year. (Do not forget to give yourself holidays!). So, say you decide on a 48-week year. Divide the annual cost by the number of working weeks. In our example that would be £3,840 divided by 48 weeks, which works out at £80 per week.

The next step is to work out the number of hours in each week actually spent making. It is important to remember that, as well as your making hours, your working week will also include time spent on paperwork, selling, answering the phone, travelling, business correspondence, etc., and that this time must somehow be charged for. The simplest way is to calculate the percentage of time in an average week you spend actually making. "Making" means all the activity directly related to actually producing the craft object. For our example, let us presume that 60% of the time is actually spent making. (A point to note is that the less time you spend making, the more you will have to charge for what you do produce, and that if you end up spending too little time making, your workshop business will probably fail).

Having calculated the percentage of time actually spent making, we can now take the weekly overhead cost and calculate an hourly rate. For this calculation, presume that you work a 40-hour week. (You will probably work a lot more than 40 hours, but if you cost your work on the basis of an 80-hour week you will have to work 80 hours *every* week to survive). If you work more hours you should make extra profit. In our example we reckon to spend 60% of the time making. On the basis of a 40-hour week that means 24 hours (60% of 40) each week are spent making.

We calculated the weekly overheads to be £80. If we divide this by the making hours in the week (which we have worked out to be 24), this gives us the hourly overhead rate of £3.35 (80 ÷ 24).

Okay so far? Good. Now let us look at the other ingredients.

LABOUR

This is what you want to earn. You know roughly what you need to live on, what your personal bills are and what style of living you would like to grow accustomed to. The simplest way to calculate an hourly labour cost is to decide how much you would hope to earn in the year. For our example, we will decide we would like to earn £6,000 a year. We have already decided to calculate on the basis of a 48-week year. So again we divide the annual sum by the working weeks to give a weekly charge (£6,000 ÷ 48 = £125 a week). To work out the hourly rate which needs to be charged to ensure that you earn your £6,000 a year, again divide the weekly charge by the making hours, which in our example we have already calculated to be 24 hours. Thus the hourly labour rate is £125 ÷ 24, which is £5.20.

MATERIALS

These are straightforward. You charge on to each object the cost of the raw materials required to make it. If you are making a batch of objects, you simple divide the total cost by the number of objects to give the material cost per object.

CONTINGENCY/PROFIT

This is another simple calculation. Once you have worked out the object cost, taking into account the overheads, labour and materials, a flat percentage is added to cover such unknowns as breakages, unexpected bills, etc. At best it may also mean that you make a little more than your hoped-for basic earnings. The flat percentage might, for example, be 15% but perhaps less on higher-priced objects.

Having worked out the hourly overheads and labour rates, all you now need to calculate is how long an object takes to make to do the final costing. As examples, let us look at a pottery jug and a silver bracelet:

Costing of jug

Let us presume that on average it takes 40 minutes to make four jugs, 20 minutes to glaze and decorate them and 20 minutes as a proportion of the time spent firing the kiln. Therefore the making time for one jug is 20 minutes (1 hour 20 minutes ÷ 4).

Overheads ⅓ (= 20 minutes) of hourly rate @ £3.35	1.10
Labour ⅓ (= 20 minutes) of hourly rate @ £5.20	1.75
Materials	50
Making price	3.35
Contingency/profit (15%)	50
Cost price of jug (excluding any VAT)	£3.85

Costing of bracelet

Let us presume that it takes 16 hours to make the bracelet.

Overheads 16 hours @ £3.35	53.60
Labour 16 hours @ £5.20	83.20
Materials (silver)	25.60
Making price	162.40
Contingency/profit (10%)	16.20
Cost price of bracelet (excluding any VAT)	£178.60

DISCOUNT

This is a reduction in price offered to encourage quicker payment. Even small discounts can encourage customers to pay promptly and many shops pay out first on invoices that carry a discount. However, do not offer a discount unless you have adjusted your cost price.

If a 10% discount is being offered for repayment within one month of delivery you need to add on 1/9th of the cost price thus:

	Original cost price	1/9th to take account of discount	Revised cost price
Jug	£3.85	£0.42	£4.27 + VAT if appropriate
Bracelet	£178.60	£19.84	£198.44 + VAT if appropriate

Thus, if the bill is settled promptly, you will receive your basic cost price, whereas if the customer is slow to pay you receive an extra amount to compensate you for the delay.

Having arrived at the cost price (sometimes referred to as the trade or wholesale price when selling to shops), you should base your selling price on this cost price.

USING THE COST PRICE TO CALCULATE THE SELLING PRICE

In different selling situations you may choose to sell at different prices, and here we look at how this might operate. One general point is that you may decide to charge a far higher price for an exceptional object. Thus the price put on a special piece may have no relation to the time spent making it. However, as a general rule the following points should be considered.

Selling to shops

This will normally be done at the cost price and the shop will then add on its mark-up to cover its costs. This will normally result in a selling price to the customer of double or more the cost price. Some craftspeople find the mark-up system difficult to understand, but you must remember that the shop must cover its own costs and is providing a service and an expertise in marketing which is valuable. If the shop sells your work on a regular basis, then it will free you from many of the problems of marketing your work and thereby release more of your time for making. If the shop is taking your work on a sale-or-return basis, then you should expect its commission to be less than if it were buying the work outright.

Selling through exhibitions

In most situations a commission is charged by the gallery and your selling price should take this into account. If you are having to pay some or all of the exhibition costs, this should also be costed in. You should expect the commission to be reduced in relation to the amount you are having to pay towards the exhibition.

If a gallery is paying all the costs and charging you 60% commission, then you might well decide to price the work at the cost price plus the 60%. In the example of the bracelet, this would mean pricing it at £285 (£178.60 plus 60% of that).

If you are having to pay £200 towards the exhibition and therefore only 30% commission, you would probably work out how many pieces you thought would be likely to sell and calculate on the basis of that. So, for example, let us say that you reckon to sell four pieces of jewellery all at roughly the same cost price as the bracelet. The simple way would be to take the cost price, add on the 30% commission and then a quarter of the actual cost, for example £50, which would give a selling price of £282.

Selling direct to the public

If you only occasionally sell to the public and normally sell through shops, then charge the public the normal shop selling price. This has two advantages. First, it stops the shops from feeling that you are undercutting (a feeling that could lead to them refusing to stock your work) and, second, it means more profit for you. You might decide to give a small discount, say 10%, for people coming direct to you. If you normally sell direct from your workshop, then it is up to you to decide what to charge. Visits by the public will interrupt your making, so it is certainly worth selling at more than cost price as a compensation.

Selling through craft fairs

Given that you will have to hire the stall and travel there (although you may cost this into your overheads), selling at more than cost price is probably a good idea. Again it is sensible to charge the normal shop retail price.

VAT

If you are registered for VAT, you must add VAT to all sales. VAT is discussed in detail on page 25.

COSTING FOR COMMISSIONS

Costing for commissions is basically the same, except that you will have to estimate the time it will take and the cost of materials in advance. Given that it is all too easy to under-estimate these and so end up making a loss on commissions, be careful and, if anything, over-estimate. If in the end it takes less time, then that will mean more profit. Also remember to charge for the design time.

When calculating what materials you require, allow for wastage and be aware of the quantities in which you may have to order. You may have to buy or hire special tools. These are all costs which you should not absorb.

Establish carefully any items, such as VAT, which are based on a rate which may change. If you are liable for VAT, always give figures exclusive of VAT, stating this is so.

You will incur other incidental expenses. You may have to make site visits, attend planning meetings or undertake special research. If you are working with other people, such as architects, you may have to consult them frequently. Should they happen to be in America, your telephone bill could be spectacular! You should itemise these additional expenses, beyond any usual reasonable workshop costs, which the client may then agree to pay as chargeable extras.

Allow a sum for contingencies. Things can always go wrong and it is better to have some room to manoeuvre. Don't forget that you may have to make special arrangements for delivery and, unless they are to be charged separately, you must include these costs in the price.

If you are confident in the accuracy of your costing, having made suitable allowance for unforeseen eventualities, you can submit a quotation to yor client rather than an estimate. This might be an important "selling point" in convincing the client that the commission should go ahead, since there will be no additional costs. But be careful as you will have to carry the cost of any overspending.

While there is no hard-and-fast legal definition of a "quote" or "estimate", it is generally agreed that a "quote/quotation" is a firm commitment to produce the object at the price stated, whereas an "estimate" is merely a fair guess and allows for flexibility in the final price.

A safer course if you are unsure of certain factors in the costing is to give some parameters (not more than £x and not less than £x).

With experience, knowing how and what to charge becomes easier. It never becomes less important. No matter how good the design and execution of your work, if you cannot get your costing right you will either lose money, which can be painful, or lose business by being unreasonably expensive, which is unnecessary. Experience of analysing each commission will improve the accuracy of your estimating, helping you to compete without being unprofitable.

Commission example: costing of table

Initial design fee: 14 hours @ £8.55	120.00
4 hours (site visits) @ £8.55	35.00
	£155.00

When you are deciding what to charge for design time, you should probably charge an hourly rate covering both labour and overheads. Remember that while you are designing you will not be making.

Making of table

Overheads (3 weeks): 72 hours @ £3.35	241.20
Labour (3 weeks): 72 hours @ £5.20	374.40
Materials	118,80
	734.40
Contingency (20%)	146.00
	£880.00 (excluding VAT)

When you are deciding on the hours, it pays to be over-cautious. If you reckon it will take just over two weeks, cost as though it will take three weeks, thereby giving yourself leeway.

Thus you would charge an initial design fee of £155, and would estimate the actual making to cost not less than £880 and not more than £1,000. You might therefore quote £900 exclusive of VAT.

MARKET RESISTANCE

While the selling price may vary depending on how and to whom you are selling, never forget the importance of not selling at less than cost price. To do so means that you earn less than you need; if you continue to sell all your work at less than what it costs to make, your workshop business will probably fail.

Of course, when people start saying they think your work is over-priced, the temptation is to lower the price. As an excuse for selling at less than cost price, many makers say that they are only doing it temporarily to encourage the person they are selling to to buy more in the future. While this can, in exceptional cases, be a valid reason, you have to be careful not to get into a situation where the buyer will always expect to buy at that price level.

Still, given the difficulties of selling craft work, which by its very nature tends to appear expensive, there may well be market resistance to your work on the ground of its price and it is worth looking at some possible ways of answering the problem. But, before doing so, stop and consider if price is the real problem. When work does not sell, the normal reaction is to presume that price is the problem but this may not necessarily be so. However, if it is, what are the possible answers?

Try other markets. It may be that the selling outlet believes that the object is over-priced, while another venue might think the price reasonable. Similary, a different clientele may have other views on what the object is worth.

Try selling it for more rather than less. Believe it or not, there is a pottter who has found that some of his work which will not sell at one price will sell really well at an even higher price! Somehow those buying the object feel it to be worth more.

Cut down on your overheads. This is not always possible, but it is worth examining your workshop and business bills to see if any savings can be made. If your workshop is large or only partly used, then sharing it with someone else could help reduce the cost to you.

Increase the inherent value. By using more expensive materials or improving the quality it is often possible to increase the selling price by far more than the increased cost of materials or making time.

Increase the percentage of time spent making. Perhaps you are not using your week efficiently and are spending too much time on other jobs. If you can increase the percentage of the week spent making, the cost of each object will be reduced.

Look at your product. Perhaps other objects would be more saleable, for example ones that are quicker and therefore cheaper to make. Some craftspeople find that an easily and quickly made range of objects can provide a bread-and-butter income which helps subsidise their own creative work. However, it is important that the quality remains high as it is quality you are selling.

Find a part-time job. Many craftsmen and women subsidise or complement their craftwork by taking part-time work. Teaching is a particularly good way of adding to your income. An alternative might be to use the workshop to make some other type of work which you know will sell well. For example, some potters produce jewellery. However, there is a danger of the other work taking over and leaving you too little time for what you really want to do.

Some craftspeople have taken to running private craft courses. Summer schools, residential weekends, etc. can earn money but they are competitive and the drawing power of your name, the venue and the popularity of the craft will all be important factors. You will have to advertise well, probably in specialist craft magazines. Running such a course will involve you in organising accommodation, catering, etc. which can be costly in terms of time and can eat into the profits.

You could also consider writing to other established private courses to see if they might be interested in hiring you as a tutor.

Local museums, arts centres, libraries and tourist centres may be interested in craft demonstrations or lectures, but be careful to receive a fee. Doing it in exchange for the chance to sell your work is often unsatisfactory; if you are demonstrating, it will be hard for you to sell at the same time.

SOME FINAL THOUGHTS

Most craftsmen and women are concerned that their work costs as much as it does. However, given that craft objects are unique objects and that few craftspeople get very rich from their craft, this concern seems misplaced. When you have to get an electrician in or get your car fixed, the hourly rate you will be charged will be far greater than you will be charging. Craftsmen and women have particular skills, normally the result of many years' training, and you should not be afraid to ask for a reasonable return for these skills.

Many craftspeople find that they can sell everything they make and yet never think of charging more. If you are able to sell everything you make, it is worth experimenting in increasing what you charge. If you become better known and your work wanted, it is not unreasonable to decide that £10,000 a year rather than £6,000 is what you want to earn and charge accordingly. Market forces determine what work can be sold for and you should not be afraid to increase your prices if the market will stand it. Many craftspeople are working 80 hours a week and selling everything they make. If they doubled their prices and as a result demand was halved, they would actually earn as much while only working 40 hours a week.

Clearly costing your work involves many factors but remember two things. Do not sell below your basic cost price and try to sell at the best possible price.

SELLING

If you are to survive it is crucial that you sell what you make. If you are considering starting up your own workshop, it is important that you have some idea of what you plan to make – the clearer, the better. Knowing what you are going to make will enable you to carry out some market research. With many craft objects it can be difficult to assess the demand, given the individuality of what is produced, until some actual selling is attempted. Before you start your business it is a good idea to produce a sample of what you plan to make to see what the response is. If you are still at college you can use the work you make there to test the market, although you must be careful that your prices accurately reflect the prices you would have to charge when paying for premises, etc. If you have not already made any work, then the best thing is to produce some, using borrowed facilities so that you can get a response before committing yourself to renting a workshop and buying expensive equipment. An enthusiastic response will give you the confidence you need to make the big step into self-employment. If there is no interest at all, then perhaps you should think again.

Whether you are starting out or are already in business, it is important that you identify the potential purchasers for your work and match your products to them. He/she is not necessarily the owner of the nearest craftshop. You should consider every possible market where someone could use or own the work you make. Look at what else is available; assessing the competition is an important part of your market research. The fact that you can make what you design often gives you an edge over those who are merely designers. Your flexibility offers you the competitive advantage of being able to provide an individual answer to a specific need.

Whether your work consist of one-off items best suited to exhibitions, large items made to commission, or batch orders requiring several sales outlets, you will need to put aside both money and time to promote sales. The budget might include paying for good photographs to circulate to galleries, the cost of a stand and attendance at a trade fair, or a professionally produced brochure aimed at prospective commissioning clients. Markets differ greatly and time would be well spent on seeking out the best potential buyers and devising the most effective method of presentation. Discovering where best to direct your promotional efforts will save you time in the long term.

Never forget that it is this individuality of design and quality of making which attracts buyers to the crafts. Craft objects can seldom compete on price terms with factory-produced objects, so emphasise the individuality of your work by putting your mark – or, better still, your signature – on every object. This emphasis should be extended to any packaging, labelling or publicity material.

SELLING FROM THE WORKSHOP

It is true that some makers successfully sell all, or the bulk, of their work direct to people visiting their workshop, but you should consider this option with care.

The main advantage is that you can set the selling price yourself as no shop mark-up is involved. (If you also sell work through shops, note the point made on selling direct on page 45). The other advantages are not having to deliver work to several outlets, and having direct contact with your customers which can provide useful feedback.

The major disadvantage is that you will have to deal with the people visiting your workshop and this can take up a lot of time and interrupt your making, in which case selling direct can become unprofitable. You will have to invest time and money in ensuring that prospective customers are attracted to the workshop, and provide a clean space for the work on sale. You will also need to consult your local planning department if you are thinking of selling direct from your workshop.

Attracting prospective customers

Research shows that people are more inclined to spend money when they are on holiday, be it a week or a day trip, so tourists can be a valuable source of sales.

Visitors to your town or area are unlikely to know their way around, so you should consider how best to help them find the workshop or shop. Talk to your local tourist office to see if details of your workshop can be included in the information they distribute; if they can be convinced that your presence will help attract more tourists to the area, then you may even be able to get some financial help to build a viewing area or sales point. Some local councils are very good at signposting, so investigate that possibility. If you decide on a poster, make sure that it is well designed and includes a simple map of where you are. Take care in siting the posters; hotels, if agreeable, are good sites, as are tourist offices and other tourist attractions. Check regularly to see that your posters are still there. Leaflets can also attract customers, although it is easy to waste money on them unless they are well directed. The Rural Development Commission or your local tourist office will be able to give advice on where best to place leaflets for maximum effect. Local newspapers are generally not so good for attracting tourists, but local radio can work fairly well.

Of course, visitors to the area will not be the only market for your work and you will also want to build up a reputation with those who live there. Word of mouth and personal recommendations count for a great deal and this needs to be encouraged by promotion. Local exhibitions, write-ups in the local press and national magazines, demonstrations at local fairs and shows all help.

When they arrive

You have to decide how to organise your space. If the workshop includes the sales area, it is best to separate the two in some way. Your display/sales area should show the work to the best advantage, and you should try to keep it and the work clean. How you present the work for sale will affect the price people will pay and their willingness to buy. High prices are unlikely to be paid if work is cluttered and dusty. Prices should be clearly marked on each piece. Information panels about the workshop, your work and yourself can save you having to answer the same questions time and time again, and details like "member of Crafts Council Selected Index" or "winner of such-and-such a prize" will encourage sales.

You will need packaging and it might be worth making this a feature. Specially printed boxes and bags, or work attractively packaged, can help sales. Many people are attracted by bargains so a "seconds" area is often a money-spinner.

If you are alone in the workshop, you will have to work out how to combine selling and making, with the minimum of disruption. People may come in to watch rather than buy and you will have to work out how best to turn visitors into customers. If a lot of people visit at once, then coping with both selling and making will become almost impossible and you may need to get help. Given the tax advantages of employing your spouse, paying your husband or wife to deal with sales may be an answer. If identifiable periods or days are particularly busy, then it may be best to limit employed help to those times. Some makers find it best to totally separate the shop area from the workshop, with visitors able to view work being made from a slight distance – a viewing area or through a window. This arrangement means that making can go ahead without interruption, while still encouraging sales, but it depends on having someone to look after the sales area all the time.

SELLING BY POST

Postal selling is another method of selling direct. Placing advertisements in local newspapers is usually expensive, although this can encourage people to visit your workshop. However, if you have a particular product that you think might attract orders by post, then experiment with advertisements for this. If you wish to explore selling your work via national advertisements you must take account of the high cost, although a small advertisement in a national Sunday newspaper or glossy magazine may result in orders for six months so the expense would have been justified.

Whether or not you should experiment with this method will depend on what you sell and on identifying the appropriate magazine or newspaper to advertise in. Selling by post will involve you in

packing; see page 80 for advice on how to avoid breakages.
For information on COD (cash on delivery) and other postal services, obtain a copy of the 'Royal Mail Inland Compendium', avaiable free from Post Offices.

TRADE FAIRS AND EXHIBITIONS

For many makers the cost of table space at a local fair or market is their first expenditure on promotion. However, at all levels – from major international trade exhibitions to local craft markets – there are organisers eager to offer space. Exhibition organisation is an industry in its own right and, unless you know why you are taking part and are ready to take advantage of your investment, it is only the exhibition organiser who benefits. For every event ask yourself who will visit it and what they will be looking for. You can meet a great number of customers and visitors interested in your work in a short time – probably more than by any other means – and you must be properly prepared to benefit.

Your aim is to sell but much depends upon the nature of the event. You may be approaching a new market in which your work is unfamiliar, in which case the emphasis is upon presenting information and finding contacts to follow up later rather than making the bulk of your sales at the event. There are different sorts of events attracting different types of buyer, and approach and presentation must be tailored accordingly. Grand titles mean nothing and it is more important to check the number and type of visitor and records of previous sales than choose to show at the "43rd International Congress of the Multi-Dimensional Plastic Arts" just because of the title.

Apart from choosing the right event and the appropriate presentation, take note of the siting of your stand. If you are close to the main entrance visitors may take immediate notice or they may walk straight past, while stands near catering facilities may attract dirty glasses, plates and wrapping paper. If you cannot get a reasonable position think again about participating.

If you decide to show then be prepared. Making a pile of everything you produce will not work – not even at a local exhibition. Choose items of your work which most closely meet the requirements of your potential customer. A busy buyer is unlikely to spare a second glance for a poorly presented group of work, and the more professional your display the more it will attract attention.

Budget for costs over and above the hire of the space. These will include display and furnishing fittings, publicity material and promotional costs, travel and subsistence. At larger events the organisers will provide a shell stand. This may be little more than walls, possibly with a raised floor and/or a lightweight ceiling. There may be severe restrictions on painting, covering or fixing items to the walls, so your displays should probably be prefabricated and free-standing. You may want to consider additional lighting and floor covering (both are sometimes offered by the organisers). Good stand lighting should be an important element in your display. Work out the area of the stand beforehand and test the assembly and display of everything. The more pre-planning of the display you can do, the more relaxed you will be when the show starts. These events are very tiring because you must continually take the initiative with visitors and potential customers.

Make sure you are noticed among all the other exhibitors. Many makers demonstrate, particularly at smaller events. This should be done with caution. It is likely to be more effective where public relations rather than sales are the aim, because when you are demonstrating you cannot be selling or paying attention to potential customers passing the stand. An immediate process, such as raising a pot or woodturning, may draw a sufficient crowd to prevent buyers reaching you and can deter sales. Yet there is nothing more compelling than a television screen – an audio-visual display may serve you better than a demonstration. A slide presentation can illustrate your craft techniques and a short repeated video tape will act as another "salesman" by briefing passers-by about your work.

Having got potential customers to stop at your stand, there are two essentials: you may secure an order, but even if you do not, get the visitor's name and address (and possibly also what they do for a living so you can assess their purchasing potential) and have something they can take away by which to remember you and your work. You can meet customers anywhere at such events and you should always be ready to record the details. Contacts from these events are vital and can be followed up later. Equally you hope that the buyer will contact you. To help them you need some well-produced, promotional literature, preferably with an illustration. You can use this material elsewhere, of course, but it must be of a quality worth keeping. If the alternative is a pile of handwritten photocopied notes, then have nothing. Well-designed and simply printed leaflets do not need to be expensive. Resist the tendency to do everything as cheaply as possible. It will be noticed and reflect on your work.

Do some research before committing yourself to a single fair by visiting a selection and learning from the mistakes of others: look at the stands, their layout, the leaflets available, the image presented and the way each stand is run. You will see busy stands enjoying obvious success and others where disconsolate people stand alone looking bored, or sit buried in a book, newspaper or their lunch. Why? It is not necessarily the quality of the work. Either the stand is wrongly designed, the staff are uninterested or they are at the wrong event – perhaps all three!

To begin with you may make little impact at these events, and it may be better to put your effort into one large and particularly appropriate fair or exhibition rather than into several small ones. Your presence implies that you are sufficiently well organised to attend and take advantage of the event, and capable of producing the orders which you hope for. You will get a direct response, with an opportunity to learn about customers' views on the work and its place in the market you are seeking to develop. While the quality of your work will ultimately determine your success, some thought and careful planning will shorten the process and prevent time-consuming and expensive mistakes.

SELLING TO SHOPS

First of all, look around to see which shops might be interested in selling your work. Specialist craft shops vary from the ultra-traditional to the ultra-contemporary and you need to judge which seem most suited to the type of work you are producing. The Crafts Council's list of selected shops, available free, may be useful in drawing your attention to possible outlets. Of course, craft shops are not the only places to consider as outlets for your work. Fashion boutiques might be interested in jewellery and scarves, toy shops in wooden objects, kitchen shops in bowls, etc. Also, while you are looking round for possible retail outlets for your work, it is worth seeing if there are gaps in the market which you might fill by producing a specific range of work.

Given that to survive you are going to have to sell most of what you make, you will either have to find a few outlets which can sell a lot of your work or many outlets which can each sell a few items. As selling involves visits and travelling (which cost money and mean less time making), the best answer is a few retail outlets each selling a lot of work, but clearly your answer will depend on the response and your particular circumstances. The Crafts Council's survey of craftsmen and women, *Working in Crafts*, shows that those working at their craft full time have, on average, about ten retail outlets selling their work. This is an average figure, however, and twenty outlets is probably more realistic.

Initially, it is probably best to select a few shops to approach at a time. Then as your business expands you can develop more outlets. In the early stages you will need to allow quite a bit of time for visiting shops to show them your work, probably one day a week. Try and ensure that you have a good range of work at this point so that you have plenty to show.

Having decided which shops you are going to approach, write or telephone to arrange an appointment. Retailers are busy and do not like people calling in without some prior arrangement. In fact, without an appointment you will often be unable to see them. So arrange an appointment and make sure that you arrive on time. If appropriate, write a postcard or a brief note confirming the time, perhaps sending some publicity material about the work. Retailing practice varies in different areas and in some cases, such as fashion shops or department stores, you may find it extremely difficult to get appointments with buyers. Only experience will tell you the best way to approach these shops. It may be best just to arrive on the doorstep and ask to see the buyer. However, if you cannot, you need to decide quickly whether it is worth showing your work to someone else. You should find out whether you are dealing with someone who has the power to decide whether to buy or order your work. Showing work to sales assistants or subordinate members of staff can be counter-productive. If they like your work and recommend it to the owner, you have to come back and make another sales pitch. If they do not like it, they could wreck any opportunity to see the buyer at a later date by making unhelpful comments.

Think about how to present your work. If you make small items, you might find it worthwhile to have a display case which will ensure that your work is always seen in the right conditions – jewellery heaped on a counter already covered in paperwork may not look as impressive as the same work displayed in a custom-built box. Think about how you present yourself. If you are visiting a smart shop in the hope of selling them expensive pieces, looking scruffy may have an adverse effect. If you make work that is designed to be worn, wear it yourself and that way the buyer can see how it looks on someone.

Before your visit, think about what you are going to show and what you are going to say. Take along enough of your work to give a clear indication of your range. Know what each piece costs; there is nothing worse than not being able to give a precise reply when asked what the work sells for. Calculate beforehand how many pieces you can produce and in what time-span. If you are given an order, there is the danger that you will agree, in the heat of the moment, to providing far more than you can produce or in too short a time. State at the time what you can actually produce rather than phoning back the next day to say that you cannot in fact carry out what was agreed. Be confident and business-like. Presumably you believe in your work and think people will wish to buy it. Craft retailers will be more likely to buy from you if they can see a consistency and conviction in your work and yourself.

Take a supply of order forms and invoices with you. If the shop orders work on the basis of what you have shown them, write out an order detailing the price, the number and the delivery date. Give them one copy and retain the other. It may be that for some reason you are uncertain about accepting a good order. Perhaps it may conflict with workshop schedules, other delivery dates, or need materials difficult to obtain. In such circumstances rather than write an order on which you might default you could write "subject to confirmation". If they are purchasing any of the items, give them an invoice. The question of sale or return will be discussed in detail later, but one point to note here is that if you do leave work on a sale-or-return basis ensure you make a list with full descriptions and prices and ask the shop owner to sign for the work. Retain the signed list and give the shop a copy for its own use.

If you receive an order or make a sale, you will be able to go to other shops with renewed confidence. But what if they say "No"? Do not accept their "no" without question. Most craftspeople are understandably nervous about selling their work, and the normal reaction to a rejection is to presume that the person hates the work and to run for the door. However, the reason for the "no" may have nothing to do with the quality of the work; if you do not ask, you will never know the reason. So ask "Why not?", a simple question which may elicit an answer that will allow you to actually make a sale. "I don't like the colour" could be the reason, and offering to supply an alternative colour could turn the "no" into a "yes". Similarly "I don't like that style" could lead to showing a different design and a sale. "I was really looking for teapots" could lead to a further meeting to which you could take those teapots you decided not to bring along the first time. It may be that they do not have the resources to purchase work at present but expect to start buying again in a month or so. Of course, it may just be that the price is too high. The temptation is then very strong to drop the price but to sell below your cost price will mean that you end up subsidising the shop.

Do not be put off revisiting a shop that has said "no". With certain places it may take several visits before your work is accepted. Going back to a shop proves to them that you are still in business and have commitment. If it is quite simply that they do not like your work, do not be discouraged. It is simply their view and others may have a better appreciation of your greatness! However, if you try several outlets which all turn your work down, it may be worth asking someone whose judgement you trust to give you their opinion on the work.

Many shops operate on the basis of "sale or return" which means that they will only pay for goods after they have been sold. This can be a disastrous practice for makers because they are in effect being asked to provide the capital finance to stock the shop, something that should clearly be the retailer's problem. It should be up to the shop to back their judgement by buying the work outright. If you are starting out, it is often hard to avoid the practice of sale or return, but you should consider whether or not it is worth accepting it in every case. If the shop promises to be a particularly profitable or prestigious outlet, you may well feel that to give them work on sale or return is reasonable as it will create a useful future trading contact. If you are trying to encourage retailers to take work which is clearly outside their normal stock, sale or return may convince them to stock it. It is worth suggesting that the shop reduce their normal commission/mark-up as it is not taking an initial risk by buying the work outright.

If you do leave work on a sale-or-return basis, it is worth checking after a week that it is actually on display. There is little point in it being there if it is left in a box under the counter. Similarly, see that it is being well displayed. As the shop has not paid for the work, there is always the danger that they will not work so hard at selling it as they will at selling work they have paid for so try to keep an eye on it. Check at regular intervals to see if the work has been sold and if it has send an invoice. If it is not selling, offer to exchange the work for other pieces as it is bad for you and the shop for the public to see a particular item on the shelves for too long. If your work does sell and the shop wishes to stock more, it may be worth trying to insist that they now buy at least some of it, with you providing additional work on sale or return so that a better range can be displayed. It is very difficult to avoid the sale-or-return problem, but you should try to work towards outlets buying your work outright as their confidence in your selling power grows.

Remember that people who run craft shops generally do it for love rather than money. Most make very small profits and often subsidise their shops either from other sources or by paying themselves little. Do not get the idea that craft shops are out to exploit you. The request that you leave your work on sale or return is a result of their own cash flow problems, and their mark-up is merely their charge to cover overheads, service, contacts and general marketing expertise. It is for you to judge whether it is good value.

Craft shops are always looking for interesting new work to sell and it is up to you, initially at least, to go out and make your work known to them.

WORKING TO COMMISSION

The intention to make commisssions a part of your business needs careful thought. Commissioned work can be more profitable than speculative work but it does not suit everyone and calls for a highly professional approach, for what is being sold initially is only an idea and the commissioner must have confidence in the maker's ability to translate it into something tangible. It is a very individual service and new business is often dependent upon personal recommendation and the maker's reputation. The decision to undertake commissions, therefore, contains three elements; being properly organised to promote and accept commissions, the need to develop a reputation as someone who responds quickly, energetically and creatively, and the determination to succeed in a specialised field.

The commissioning contract

Central to the commissioning process is the contract with the client. The contract is an agreement for you to supply skill, materials and labour in producing an object in return for a sum of money. In its simplest form it is a verbal request by the commissioner for the work to be undertaken, but it is far more satisfactory if the agreement is *in writing*. With a simple straightforward commission, the least which should be accepted is an exchange of letters. Disputes about payment, quality, damage and a whole range of other factors may occur, and the contract protects both parties. You may find it useful to develop a standard contract, perhaps containing clauses specifically relevant to your work and in this case you would be well advised to ask a solicitor to draw up a form of agreement.

A simple contract should set out the following:

1. who the agreement is between, particularly if the commissioner is a company or organisation rather than an individual
2. what will be made, including any design specifications, e.g. dimensions. The description may also carry reference numbers to the appropriate design drawings
3. what materials will be used, with exact descriptions, such as the fineness of precious metals, if necessary
4. the fee payable
5. any time limit, or completion date for the project
6. change of ownership – it is usual to stipulate that the work remains the maker's property until receipt of final payment

Clauses 1–4 state absolutely basic information, while the time limit offers reassurance to the client that the work will be produced, and the ownership clause offers a measure of protection to the maker. The question of ownership could be important if there are problems over payment, particularly if the work might be delivered before the final payment has been received.

In addition to these the maker should consider various other clauses, depending on the nature of the commission and his/her method of working:

Design fee A commission for which a new or reworked design is required should include a clause agreeing a fee for the design work *whether or not* it is accepted. Depending upon the nature of your work, you may have a standard fee.

Materials The use of scarce, unusual or exotic materials may involve unforeseen expenditure, particularly if the job is a long one. You should consider a clause making clear the basis on which such materials will be charged. This might be at cost or as a supplement should their cost rise above an agreed figure.

Amendments After accepting your designs and work has begun, the client may wish to vary the terms of the commission. You should state the basis on which alterations will be charged. This would normally be your hourly rate for making the changes and any additional material costs. You must consider whether and how to charge for work already completed which has to be abandoned due to alterations.

Cancellations Cancellation is always a bad moment and, while it may be due to circumstances over which your client has no control, if a contract has been signed then the client will be legally bound to reimburse you for all costs incurred up to the point of cancellation. However, given the difficulty of agreeing what should be paid, a cancellation clause should be seriously considered as an essential part of any commission agreement and should outline the basis on which the calculation for your own charges will be made. A fee calculated on the number of hours worked is the simplest and most easily agreed method, although it may be necessary to relate the figure to the proportion of the commission completed at cancellation.

Arbitration This clause need only stipulate that in the event of a dispute an independent arbitrator will be agreed, or it may name the arbitrator.

Payment Misunderstandings can occur if the number, method and timing of payments are not agreed and so these must be stated. It is usual for payment to be made in three or four parts; the first when the commission is agreed, part when it is half completed and the final payment on completion and delivery. Where special or expensive materials are involved, a larger number of part-payments may be required to allow for them. If appropriate, stipulate the method of payment. It may be necessary to state in which currency the agreed fees will be paid, particularly if dealing with an overseas client. There will be less risk if the payment is made in sterling.

Delivery and installation Special arrangements may be necessary to deliver or install the work. It should be clear who will pay for any additional costs involved in delivery. Should a third party be involved in shipping or delivering the work, consideration must be given to the need for insurance and a clear statement made regarding responsibility for loss or damage during this phase.

Defects The maker has an obligation to supply goods of merchantable quality under the Sale of Goods act. However, the work may have minor imperfections and it is reasonable to specify a period, say seven days following delivery, during which any defects should be reported which would be repaired at your expense. Such a clause would guard against claims for damage caused subsequently. It is worth noting, however, that the maker remains liable for hidden defects.

Copyright (see page 74) In commissioning work most clients will assume that copyright will pass to them with the work. This should be discussed with the client and a clause agreed transferring the copyright to them if appropriate.

Chargeable extras You may wish to charge for incidental extras, such as travel expenses, over and above the fee. What is to be charged should be agreed in advance and clearly stipulated.

The commissioning process

In preparing for commissions, consider exactly what they entail for you and your methods of working. Securing an order, possibly in competition with other designers, means that you must be certain that you can discuss your work, designs, production and delivery dates with complete confidence. Be in the right place at the right time in a sufficiently unhurried state to present yourself, your work and your business as both efficient and reliable. You will need a diary and a workshop schedule to assess quickly your ability to accept work within a fixed time-scale.

Clients must be able to contact you. You should consider whether to rent or buy a telephone answering machine. If you do not have a telephone of your own, find someone who will always take messages for you, or perhaps use one of the small office service agencies. Whatever method you use, make sure that people can contact you quickly and easily – commissions rely on this.

You must be certain of up-to-date prices for materials and their availability. Iron out early problems or the client may approve designs for which you cannot get the materials you have specified.

A letter may be your first contact with a client. Although neat handwriting is quite acceptable, typing is almost always easier to read. However, even if writing by hand, use carbon paper and keep a copy; it is impossible to remember what you have written to everyone. Duplicate notebooks are useful; when you have mislaid your notes of a meeting, telephone conversation, order or any other information, you have always got a back-up copy. Keep the notes and your correspondence in a simple filing system.

Check lists are helpful to remind you at every stage of the things which are so easy to forget. They range from your needs for the first visit to a client (notebook, diary, photographs, samples, tape measure and client's address!) through to delivery of the work (essential assembly tools, duster, repair kit, notebook and tape measure in case of another commission).

Of all the meetings that you have with a client, the first is probably the most important. It is then that you establish confidence in your work and your credibility as a maker. If you are vising the client make sure that you are on time, with everything you will need. If you are late, ill-equipped or unprepared you are at a disadvantage from the start. Be clear where you have got to be – and how to get there! Have the client's telephone number handy and, if you are delayed, ring to say so.

If the client is coming to you, you should have somewhere clean and tidy to make your presentation. If the workshop does not have an area which you can keep for such meeting, you may be able to use a nearby hotel lobby or somewhere similar. But remember that pubs and other public places can be noisy and very distracting.

Both you and the client will be assessing each other at this meeting. Try and ensure that there are the fewest possible diversions to break your concentration. You will be less self-conscious if you dress to fit the occasion. A suit may be out of place if the client always wears T-shirts. It will be easier to build up a rapport with clients if you know something about them or perhaps their business, so a little research should pay dividends.

Probably you will know roughly what is wanted. Choose a small selection of photographs and/or drawings specifically for the occasion and again matched to the client. It is not necessary to run through your life's work, but a little variety with one or two unexpected designs might show something the client did not know you made and encourage additional work.

In discussing work never be afraid of saying "no". Should you be unhappy about working for the client, or feel for any reason that you cannot tackle the job, then do not go ahead. A bad commission could do you more harm than no commission. Refusing a commission may also mean taking the trouble to explain why. The personal nature of commissioning means that a careful explanation can result in the client varying the terms, possibly making the job acceptable. You could be asked to submit ideas for another commission at some future date because of the care with which you handled a refusal.

You must expect to assemble a detailed brief at the meeting. If you are visiting the client, make sure that you do not have to go back to take further measurements or ask for additional information. You should establish exactly what is wanted: dimensions, materials, colour and any specific limitations, as well as noting the style and taste of the client. You will need to know delivery dates and whether elements of the commission could be affected by other factors such as structural work or redecoration which need to be completed first.

You must establish quickly what the client is expecting to pay. If your work is simply not possible at the price, say so at once. Exciting designs may encourage an increase in the preliminary figure, but you must avoid any possible misunderstanding and be clear about the financial limitations.

It may be appropriate for you to make a separate design agreement at this stage. You might charge a standard fee, or a sum may be included in the main commission agreement. Whatever the case, you should agree with the client that you will be paid for your design work, whether it is accepted or not.

The last point is to agree the date when you will present your designs. It will be an important moment and you will want to ensure you can get everything ready, so make certain the agreed date allows for existing commitments.

While there is complete freedom to express yourself in the proposals you submit, it is fundamental that your designs must satisfy the client's brief. However well presented your ideas, the client is unlikely to proceed with the commission if you have not designed what he/she wants or needs. You can of course show additional designs and amendments in the hope of varying the brief if there is something appropriate you would particularly like to produce.

In discussing designs you may well have to protect clients from themselves. It is pointless slavishly agreeing with a client's wishes if you know that what is wanted will collapse under its own weight or draw blood every time it is worn! If you cannot get an agreement about the essential practical elements for the work, do not go ahead with the work: again, a bad commission is probably worse than no commission.

In preparing your suggestions, be conscious of the longevity of the work, as well as the need for maintenance. Future commissions and the possibility of more work will suffer if you are constantly being asked to adjust, repair or service earlier pieces.

If you are making something large for a specific place, make sure that it can be got where it will be needed. You may have to alter your designs in order to get the work through a door if you cannot assemble it on site. Even for a small item this can be a limiting factor; your client, without mentioning it, may be expecting to keep something in a safe or cupboard with restricted access.

The greatest limitation on your design will be cost, and you must change your ideas if you cannot produce them within the proposed figures. You can always draw up properly costed amendments and additions showing how the designs could be improved.

When you come to show your designs, make sure they are properly presented. It may be necessary to give the designs explanatory titles and reference numbers to avoid misunderstandings. Figures and dimensions should be noted on all the drawings, together with details of the materials to be used. If the client does not understand design drawings, you can either produce a small maquette or draw a sketch of the piece. It is always a good idea to produce samples of the materials to be used and the finishes which you have planned.

When clients approve the design you should consider asking them to note their acceptance on the appropriate drawing. If you have provided a selection from which to choose, the client's signature will prevent confusion later.

The approval of the design is a significant moment and may be the time for you and your client to sign the commission agreement. If appropriate, you can now submit the invoice for your design fee, and (on receipt of the agreed initial payment) begin production.

When production is under way the client may wish to see the work in progress. You should decide whether or not you will make a practice of this. Many makers feel clients should not see the apparent chaos of a workshop, which can discourage them. For others, demonstration of the skills and processes of production are an essential element of involving the client in the creation of an individual piece.

If for some unavoidable reason you need to alter the specification, you must consult the client. If you vary the specifications without permission the client might quite reasonably refuse to pay.

Time schedules are important. If you have agreed a date for completion of the commission you will be in breach of your contract if you do not complete it by this date. This can result in the client refusing the work and even, in certain situations, asking for compensation. This is particularly relevant if you are working as part of a larger contract – on a new building, for example – where your failure to deliver on time could hold up other contractors. Even if no specific completion date has been agreed, you must supply the commissioned work within a reasonable period of time. The relevant legislation is the Supply of Goods and Services Act 1982. If you are being commissioned by an architect on a building project, you may be asked to work as a sub-contractor to the main building contractor, and it is likely that such a contract will contain penalty clauses which can be severe if delays occur in delivering the commissioned work. It is advisable to try and steer clear of such a contract and instead try and be contracted directly by the architect.

If you do run into difficulties with a piece, always inform the client of any potential delay. It is never easy making excuses for being late, but it helps if you have given warning that it is likely to happen.

Whether production is on schedule or not, you should let your client know when it is nearly complete. Completion may involve the client in getting ready to receive the work or, perhaps more important, in making arrangements to have the money ready to pay you. In any case, advance warning at this stage should heighten anticipation of the eagerly awaited delivery.

Having advised the client that the work is almost ready, arrange delivery only when it is complete. There can always be last-minute snags for both you or your client. The details of responsibility and costs for this stage should have been agreed long ago, but you should plan the delivery or installation in detail.

Make sure that you have test-assembled everything and that you have sufficient people to help you. Your reputation could be severely dented if you turn up expecting your client's family to manhandle heavy items into some confined space. You must have the necessary tools for assemly with you, as well as a kit to repair or retouch any minor damage on the spot. Be prepared to take advantage of the success of the commission to develop another, possibly having thought about a companion piece, and be equipped to take notes and measurements as necessary.

It is important to recognise that the delivery or installation of the commission is a crucial moment for your client. It may be that with a little imagination or some extra expenditure you can make the first sight, or unveiling, win an additional advantage. The pleasure of experiencing the new commission can be ruined if it is badly presented, and for your client the climax of the process should be taking possession of the work.

Payment

Don't be reticent about discussing money – you can't survive without it. If you have discussed payment from the outset and both parties are clear about the costs involved, there should be no confusion. The commission agreement should state when payments are due. It is then up to you to submit your invoices at the appropriate stages. You cannot expect the client to pay without them.

Because of the particular nature of commissions, you should guard against proceeding with work at any stage if payment is over-due or you have reason to believe it could be withheld. In the event of non-payment, obviously some commissioned work can still be saleable. However, if you keep going without receiving the agreed payments, you may find that your reward is possession of something which is totally unsaleable to anyone other than your defaulting client.

Learning to talk about money with confidence and making sure that you do not carry out more work than necessary without payment are important factors in commissions. You cannot develop a business without taking some risks, but you can keep them to a minimum.

Developing commissions and getting work

If commissioned work is to be developed as a significant proportion of your production, a specialised promotional approach will probably be necessary. It takes considerable time to build up a reputation to the point where commissions are self-generating. In addition to being organised to take commissions, you must also be able to make a specific appeal to the clients who are likely to commission you.

It may be appropriate to produce simple, concise and well-illustrated promotional material. This should show the range of your work and the type of commissions which you undertake, as well as implying your competence and ability to work to commission. Such material can be used in a variety of ways to place your name and services before potential clients.

Some types of work may be sufficiently straightforward for promotional material and the commissioning agreement to be combined as an illustrated order form. Should this be the case, it is important that clients have space and suitable guidance to set out their instructions very clearly. However, this will only be appropriate for more repetitive work where the terms and conditions are standard.

If you have promotional material you will need to plan carefully how best to circulate it. There are many professional organisations, such as RIBA or SIAD, for architects, interior designers, the advertising industry and others, through whom you might contact those most likely to be interested in what you make. In addition, many of these organisations maintain records of people who can be commissioned to provide a variety of services. It is worth making sure that details of you and your work are included wherever it might be of potential benefit. Often this can be done without cost. Specialised services, such as the Crafts Council's Index of Makers, are always useful, particularly when they are publicised as aids to commissioning work. For any such service you should make every effort to meet the criteria for selection in order to take advantage of the additional publicity.

To gauge more immediately reactions to the service you offer, you could assemble a carefully chosen selection of names from the appropriate categories of a local directory such as Yellow Pages and send them the information. By following this up with a telephone call and perhaps a visit, you will get a direct response and be able to judge which sections of the market are or are not likely to be worth pursuing. Remember the personal nature of commissioning. When contacting organisations, groups or companies, always try and identify the appropriate individual and write to them by name and not by title or job description.

It should now be apparent why the professionalism of your promotional material is essential. If your first approach is through the letterbox, you must send something which is both interesting and worth retaining. Handwritten photocopies are worthless, yet people still try and use them.

As your reputation grows, your fee for working to commission can be expected to rise. You may well plan to attract work in the early days by keeping charges low but remember never to work below cost price. You must guard against getting a reputation for being too cheap. It is a sure recipe for going out of business. A reputation for creativity and reliability is what you need.

There may be commissions that are so important for the development of your business that you will deliberately put forward unprofitable estimates. Such a loss can, of course, be construed as a promotional cost. An opportune, well-executed commission which loses money may establish your credibility with a client and open the door to a great deal of highly profitable work. You must gauge the long-term benefits carefully and take the gamble if it seems right, but don't plan to do it too often.

There are an increasing number of competitions for commissions. In some areas, such as architecture, it is expected that submissions will be on a purely speculative basis and no design fees are payable. It is important therefore when considering entry to a competition that you are quite certain of the terms under which it is being held. When no rejection fees are payable, you must estimate the cost to your business if your designs are not selected. Competitions can be worth entering, but they require extra effort if your work is to have a chance of selection. With this in mind you must consider not only the loss in unpaid design time if you are not successful, but also whether the competition is worth winning.

It may be that the nature of your work would allow a shop, gallery or other agent to attract business and undertake some of the negotiating on your behalf. You are probably a better designer and maker than promoter, and you should be aware of the benefits of getting others to help you attract work. Much will, of course, depend upon identifying appropriate shops or galleries who are sympathetic to your work and prepared to make a positive effort to encourage and promote a commissioning service.

As with other forms of retailing, it is perfectly reasonable for the agent or retailer to take a commission for promoting and selling your work. The amount will depend upon what they do. With your agreement, some may undertake initial negotiations, handling all the financial arrangements and dealings with the client, for which a fee of not less than 25% of the total commissioned figure is perfectly reasonable. Similarly, expect to pay an introductory fee of around 10% to any agent bringing business to you – even if you undertake all the dealings with the client yourself. Remember that this is work you would not have without someone else's efforts and be ready to include such fees in your estimates, regarding them as the cost of increased business, *not* reduced profits.

A more difficult problem is that of repeat fees should you be approached directly by a client for a further commisson. If an agent is actively promoting your work, he or she may well have played a part in the repeat order coming about. You should perhaps consider an arrangement whereby the agent receives a fee (say 5%) of any repeat business from a client within one or two years of the original commission. Again, it is a reasonable reward for finding you a good client. Whatever procedures you adopt, you should always find some way of repaying those who promote your work and introduce business to you – your next commission might depend on it.

As your promotional efforts begin to bring in work, remember to keep a proper record of successful commissions. It is worth investing in good photographs, particularly when you are pleased with the results of a commission. You can take your own photographs but they must be good. Bad photographs do you and the work no credit and should never be used. Promotional material can be greatly improved if you are able to include a well-illustrated case history which demonstrates clearly your ability to deliver the finished article.

The story of an interesting commission together with good photographs may attract magazine coverage. All such articles help build a reputation and offer a chance for further promotion. It may be worth paying for a run-on of the pages illustrating your work to send out with your promotional material to prospective clients. The more important the magazine, the more its reputation will assist you.

You should also be aware of the value of secondary publicity, You may have used specialist materials, tools or techniques. Always inform trade and technical journals who may be interested in some aspect of a commission. Perhaps your work used an unusual timber; photographs and details of the work sent to the marketing director of the timber importers, or even the commercial attaché at the embassy of the timber's country, may well give you substantial additional publicity if they highlight your commission for their own promotional purposes. Similarly, the work may have been produced using new tools, techniques or specialist skills which will be of interest to a far wider range of people than you would consider. Examine every opportunity where publicity, however obscure, can put details of your work before a new audience.

In circulating publicity and seeking promotion, do not forget that the nature of commissioning may have given you access to confidential information. Quite apart from the question of copyright, which you must consider, you should get the client's agreement before you circulate details of his/her property. Your photographs could inadvertently show the siting of the office safe or the burglar alarm system!

Provided that your clients are agreeable, it does no harm to circulate details of recent commissions at regular intervals. Repeat business is important and this information shows your newer work to those who have commissioned you before and demonstrates the demand for your services. They will probably enjoy hearing of your continued and growing success, which after all flatters their judgement in commissioning you in the first place, and may lead to them placing a further order.

Commissions come in all shapes and sizes. They can range from a small job for an individual to major pieces of work for large companies and local authorities. The scale of your response will depend upon the nature of the work. What is always important is the speed with which you respond. Commissions, more often than not, are won or lost on the enthusiasm and professionalism of your initial reply. In building your reputation and business, remember that it is your ability to react quickly that offers you a major advantage over and above your creative skills. You must be ready and willing to take that advantage.

LEGAL POINTS

Contracts

A contract, or binding legal agreement, may be verbal or written. With very few exceptions, a verbal contract is as binding as a written one. However, the problems arise when it is necessary to prove what was agreed verbally and this is why it is advisable that all business contracts should be in writing. The most obvious contracts which craftsmen or women make are contracts for the purchase of materials and services from suppliers, or contracts for the sale of finished objects or services to shops and galleries or to members of the public. These contracts, which could be verbal but are better in writing, might be in the form of an invoice or a letter, but in any case should cover a number of standard points: the names of the buyer and seller, the items bought and sold, the price, the delivery date, place of delivery and any discount arrangements – but there may be many other terms which should be written down to prevent disagreements later. The parties to the agreement will also be bound by a number of statutory requirements designed mainly to protect the consumer.

Sale of Goods Act 1979

This act lays a number of obligations on both buyer and seller which come into operation in any contract for the sale of goods when the buyer and seller have not made a definite agreement on the various points. Some of the main obligations for a seller are:
(a) That the goods sold are of "merchantable quality", i.e. are capable of doing what a buyer might reasonably expect them to do: a chair which collapses when sat upon would fail this test.
(b) The goods must be fit for any particular purpose made known to the seller. Thus, if a buyer asks "Can this garment be machine washed?", the seller will be held responsible for the reply.
(c) The goods must correspond with the seller's description of them, for example, a jug described as "a 3 pint jug" must hold 3 pints.
(d) If the buyer has not examined the goods before delivery, he/she must be given a reasonable opportunity to do so.
If the goods fail any of the tests above, the buyer is entitled to reject them, and be refunded in full.

Supply of Goods and Services Act 1982

This act extends many of the conditions set out in the Sale of Goods Act to contracts for the supply of services. Thus, in the absence of any express agreement between the parties, the following conditions apply: the work will be carried out with reasonable care and skill, within a reasonable time, and the customer will pay a reasonable charge. Although the act is useful, it is naturally much more business-like to establish both parameters of time and charges before the job commences.

Trade Descriptions Acts 1968-1972

Under these it is also a criminal offence deliberately to mis-describe your goods whether verbally or in writing, including advertisements. A trade description covers such things as quality, method of manufacture, composition, fitness for the purpose, and the person who made it.

Unfair Contract Terms Act 1977

This act was passed to prevent traders or suppliers slipping unfair exclusion clauses into contracts, typically in small print on the back of an invoice. Such clauses as "the maker accepts no responsibility whatsoever for any defects" no longer have much force, for it is up to the seller to prove that the exclusion clause is fair and reasonable in the circumstance.

Consumer Protection Act 1961

This act makes it an offence to sell or hold in stock any items which are covered by a series of regulations made under the act which are designed to protect the consumer from death or injury. Of particular relevance to craftspeople are the regulations for toys, glazed ceramic ware (if designed for use with food or drink) and domestic electrical equipment. The penalties for non-compliance are severe, so makers should ensure that they have carried out the tests required by the regulations.

In addition, and this applies to any manufactured item, if a consumer or user comes to any harm as a direct result of the negligence of the maker, or even of the designer, he/she can sue for damages.

Hallmarking Act 1973

Hallmarking was introduced in 1273 and today it still ensures that a purchaser of a gold, silver or platinum item will not be defrauded. Every jeweller making work for sale must ensure that it is properly marked. The other side of the case, however, which causes a good deal of trouble for experimental jewellers is that an object, for example, made of gold with a small addition of decorative iron must not be hallmarked as gold. Indeed it is against the law even to describe it as gold and such a piece would have to be labelled "yellow metal and iron".

Sale or return

This special type of sales contract is so common in the crafts world that it is worth noting the particular legal characteristics. Here, although the goods have passed from the maker into the possession of the shop/gallery, the ownership of the goods remains with the maker. As a consequence, the maker can take back the goods at any time; any risk to the goods (in the absence of negligence by the shop) also remains the responsibility of the maker, who should insure accordingly. It also follows that when a sale to a member of the public finally takes place, the sale is technically between the maker and the ultimate buyer. The shop/gallery will have acted as agent for the sale and will charge the maker a commission for its services; VAT will be chargeable only on this commission. Because of these peculiarities, as well as the purely practical difficulties of keeping track of items out on sale or return, it is essential to maintain proper paperwork and to incorporate into the contract of sale or return with the gallery a clause altering the implied condition about risk mentioned above. Such a clause might read "The gallery/shop shall reimburse the maker for any loss or damage to the goods from whatever cause while in the possession of the gallery/shop".

Debt collection

Craftspeople who in general supply in small quantities are in an extremely vulnerable position when it comes to collecting their debts. If goods have been supplied on sale or return, it may take the maker many weeks of pestering and finally a visit even to discover that a piece of work has been sold by the shop and that he/she is therefore owed the price less the commission. And then (and this applies to outright sales as well) if the retailer fails to pay, the maker will have to decide whether to take legal action over a small sum of money. For a sum of, say, £30 it is hardly worth the legal fees, anxiety and sheer loss of making time. There is no answer to a most unfair situation once it has got to this stage. The real answer lies in being confident of the honesty of the retailer. Ask colleagues who already supply the outlet what their experience has been – does the retailer look after the work, pass back information on sales regularly and pay bills promptly.

If it does come to a court action it is now possible to take action yourself in the County Court. This is a fairly easy process and the court officials should help you to fill in simple forms which are required to issue a summons against your debtor. Full details of the process are contained in the leaflet "Small Claims in the County Court: how to sue and defend actions without a solicitor", available free from County Court offices. The other alternatives are to use debt collecting agencies, which are quite effective but charge a percentage of the debt collected, or to instruct solicitors.

Copyright

The copyright laws seek to prevent "artistic works" and "works of artistic craftsmanship" from being copied without the permission of the owner of the copyright.

Craftspeople are at a slight disadvantage compared to fine artists as regards this part of the law. Whereas fine artists whose work falls into the category of "artistic works" (drawing, paintings, sculptures, engravings and photographs) are afforded copyright protection regardless of artistic merit, craftspeople have to show not only craftsmanship but also artistic intent in order to obtain protection for their objects. For this reason, craftspeople who feel at risk of being plagiarised should keep the drawings from which the objects were made, for the drawings will automatically have protection as "artistic works".

Copyright arises automatically with the creation of the work and no formalities or registration are required. It is wise however to sign every drawing or object with the international copyright symbol ©, your name and the date. The normal rule is that the maker becomes the first owner of the copyright and it is worth noting that even if a work has been sold, unless there is an agreement to the contrary, copyright remains with the maker. The right lasts for the life of the creator and for 50 years thereafter. The creator can of course grant a licence for someone else to copy the work, or can assign (in writing) the copyright in full.

Designs which are mass-produced (i.e. over 50 copies) or which are registered under the Registered Designs Act 1949, and which are judged solely by their outward appearance, receive protection similar to that under copyright law, but for 15 years only.

The Chartered Society of Designers, 29 Bedford Square, London WC1B 3EG, publish useful guides on design protection, copyright, etc.

Trade marks

A trade mark is a symbol, which might be a signature, logo, monogram or words, by which goods are identified as being made or supplied by you. They can be registered at the Register of Trade Marks but it seems unlikely that many craftspeople will find this fairly expensive process useful. In any case, if other people try to pass off their objects as yours, you could probably sue them under Common Law.

EXPORTING

It is important to make a distinction between exporting as a business, compared to the technicalities of sending work abroad on one or two occasions. If you are determined to develop markets for your work overseas, then exporting should be a specific and planned element of your business for which you have clear and justifiable reasons. It will require time and money as well as a considerable amount of research and preparation. Without these, your efforts at exporting are likely to be buried beneath a mountain of paperwork or cripple you with unexpected costs.

If a friend returning from holiday comments "I saw one just like yours selling for five times the price", this is not a general signal to load the car and head for the nearest ferry. Nor is the knowledge that someone else's work has sold well abroad or an inability to sell your work at home sufficient reason for believing you should be exporting. Selling abroad is likely to be more difficult than selling at home. However, you may be offered the opportunity of an exhibition abroad or an overseas visitor to your workshop may show interest in your work and ask you to send some examples. You may be going on holiday and feel that it would be a useful opportunity to see whether there is any interest in what you make. In each case, you need to solve the practical difficulties of getting work abroad. It is important to recognise that as a single operation the time and costs involved may well make it unprofitable, although there are of course many other compensations, not least the satisfaction of having one's work exhibited or sold in other countries.

Before dealing with the practical problems of shipping* craft work, it would be useful to consider some aspects of the more formal development of exporting as part of your business.

The first essential principle is to concentrate your effort. Certainly, it would be very nice to have your work spread throughout five continents but even the giant multi-nationals have enough difficulty achieving this. You are seeking to develop a market in a different culture with a different language. Probably in a different time zone, with sizes in metric units and where the value of money changes every day in relation to the pound, quite apart from differing from country to country. Under these circumstances, even the EEC as part of Europe is too diverse an area for you to tackle all at once. You would be best advised to pick a single country, or even a region within that country, where you have reason to believe that your work will attract a response and, having researched further, concentrate all your efforts on making a success of that market. If success comes, then growth and a further spread of your work will follow naturally.

---

* "Shipping" is the general term used to describe sending work abroad.

RESEARCH

The formal channels for developing marketing research for exports are often inappropriate for the individual craftsperson. Naturally they tend to relate to clearly established product categories, and being told that a certain percentage of a gross national product is spent on giftware is of little value to you. The crafts seldom feature in such statistics and if they do it is often as a subdivision of a general giftware heading. But you are not looking for market research information about interest and opportunities in a general crafts market; you need to know whether there is specific interest in what you make and this is best obtained from those selling, or perhaps even making, similar pieces in the country in which you are interested.

For individual pieces of work, arts magazines, the magazines and newsletters of national craft organisations, specialist guild and society newsletters throughout the world all have advertisements, exhibition reviews and other editorial material in which details and addresses of specialised shops and galleries are given. Illustrations in gallery advertisements are a useful indicator of the style of work which is of interest to them.

The Department of Trade & Industry (DTI)* in London, or through their regional offices, has information regarding commercial attachés, trade development officers and other staff abroad. The British Council should be able to provide details of their officers or embassy cultural attachés for the country in which you are interested. Rather than approach the organisations in this country, which will only carry more general information,, you can then write abroad with specific and detailed enquiries. It is pointless asking the British Council or any similar organisation for general information, such as a list of galleries throughout Europe and America, but if you ask for details of galleries in Baden-Baden or a list of craft fairs in New York State, it is more than likely that you will get a useful reply. The more specialised your questions, the easier it is for them to be answered or for you to be given details of someone who can help you with information.

Your research may need to include other factors. Remember that goods imported into other countries often require specific marking or labelling, so it may be necessary for you to have wording such as "Made in England" on every piece. You will also have to consider whether your work could be affected by product liability conditions or legally imposed safety standards. This would particularly apply to toys and electrical goods. The fittings on your lamp bases may need to be labelled that they are of an approved type or meet the required standard. Extra shipping documents may be required. Some goods such as cheap, mass-produced textiles which have special duty or

* For addresses of relevant organisations, see page 86.

import restrictions can affect similar categories of work. Most countries therefore require a certificate showing the country of manufacture for textiles of any type, even a single wallhanging. Such certificates of origin are issued by the Chambers of Commerce. The DTI can advise on product specifications, legal and marking requirements.

You can do a lot of research and indeed make sales to overseas buyers without leaving this country. Many of the larger overseas department stores and chains of shops have buying agencies here, usually in London. Not all want mass-produced work and approaching them can be an excellent way of testing foreign interest in your work. If you are successful, it is usual for them to undetake all the shipping and necessary documentation, paying you in sterling as soon as you fulfil their order as if selling in this country., The buying houses usually act for countries which are further afield, as European buyers can visit this country more easily. The Export Buying Offices Association can give details of the agencies for the country in which you are interested. A point to remember is that the buying houses themselves do not usually make the decision to purchase. They collect information, samples and all appropriate details about the work so that all the background research is done before store buyers come to this country, on their purchasing trips. Although they are not the decision makers, they are usually well briefed in the likes and dislikes of the stores for which they act, the types of market served and the sales potential of the work that they see. So even if you are not successful in selling to them, you may get useful background information as to the likely appeal of your work in the country you are trying to tackle.

PRICING AND COSTING TERMS

Before sending any work abroad, you must first consider how you are going to be paid. If pieces are going to an exhibition or on sale or return, make quite certain you know, and have agreed, the prices at which the work will be offered before it is sent. Preferably the agreement should be in writing, but if this is not possible before the shop or gallery has seen the work you must at least be clear about the rates at which commission or mark-up will be applied and who will organise and pay for the return of the unsold work. You should have agreed how the shipping costs will be met and the method of payment. Do not let your enthusiasm at being offered an overseas exhibition make you forget basic business practices. Once your work has left this country, you could have considerable difficulty in getting it either paid for or returned. You can ask for a banker's reference, or for a single operation it may be possible to make *ad hoc* arrangements between your respective banks regarding the transfer of funds, possibly by banker's draft, without having to resort to the more formal method of documentary credits. However, if you are looking to develop exporting in any serious way then export financing must be thoroughly investigated.

You will need to be familiar with some of the ways of quoting costs to overseas buyers. Unless they are visiting you in this country and making payment in sterling, they will probably want you to estimate the "landed costs". These represent the cost of your work plus customs duties and taxes, and specific elements of the shipping costs, usually up to arrival in the foreign country. You would be unwise ever to quote prices which include final delivery to a purchaser abroad (other than by post) since these would also include local transportation costs as well as any customs duties and taxes which have to be paid. It is best to quote (possibly in foreign currency) in one of the following ways:

1. Ex-works. This is the basic cost of your pieces as if someone were collecting them from your workshop.

2. FOB (free on board). This is a comprehensive costing, including your ex-work price plus packaging and the cost of getting the shipment to an agreed port or airport of departure and loaded on the ship or aircraft. You would therefore quote "FOB Harwich" or "FOB Gatwick".

3. C & F (cost and freight). This costing details the price of the work and its carriage to the agreed point of arrival, which can be a port or an inland airport, for example "C & F Chicago".

4. CIF (cost, insurance and freight). This is the same as C & F with the addition of insurance costs for the consignment.

Taxes and customs duties vary from country to country. Even within the Common Market, where no duties are payable on goods passing between member countries, VAT rates vary. Entering other EEC countries, VAT will be payable on your work whether you are registered for VAT in this country or not. Taxes and customs duties can affect the price of your work abroad in a way which you cannot control.

Bearing in mind the constant change of rates of exchange, unless you have made careful calculations you would be well advised initially to quote prices in sterling. However when doing business or attending trade events in other countries it is important to have prepared detail prices in the local currency. It is unlikely that you will be operating on a scale to take part in any of the export credit funding arrangements, but formal quotes and orders are important. A written order confirming a proposed purchase by an overseas buyer could be very useful in discussing finance with your bank manager! If you have taken the trouble to get the initial stages correct, you are likely to find other people much more helpful in solving the practical problems of getting your work shipped abroad.

Finally, if you seriously want to develop an export market, your work, its price, the way you distribute and sell it, and your promotional effort should from the outset be designed for and compatible with your buyer's market conditions rather than the pattern at home. Exporting may seem nothing but a mass of problems but many overseas markets are larger or more profitable than ours, and once you have made your first attempt the contacts and experience gained will make subsequent efforts easier.

HOW TO DO IT

Customs and shipping procedures operate to a set of rules and the more you conform to standard procedures, the easier life will be.
It is essential that you leave yourself sufficient time to find out what procedures are necessary before you arrive at a critical deadline – do not arrive at the dock gates with the boot of a car filled with individual objects which you claim to be valuable works of art or you are liable to complicate your life beyond your worst nightmares.

A major problem is that international documentation has no category to cover that all-embracing word "crafts". It depends upon the country involved whether work can be categorised as "works of art", and this is more than likely carefully defined so that subjective judgements are avoided. Customs officers have to operate the rules and you cannot expect them to be altered for you. If you appear unprepared or unhelpful, or expect customs officers to make artistic judgements about your work you will run into problems. They are used to dealing with businesses familiar with customs procedures, whose documents have been carefully prepared in advance. Quantity and value may well be significant, so check what is allowed duty free. You can take some objects abroad as samples or within your personal gift allowance but don't expect to get away with six full tea chests. You might be allowed a single piece of furniture simply as a household effect but have difficulty taking a single piece of very expensive jewellery. Use your common sense but do not expect help if you deliberately set out to ignore or break the law or internationally agreed procedures.

Packing work

You must ensure work is properly packed. More money is lost through bad packing than almost any other cause and it is advisable to buy proper packing materials, including their price in your export costings. Look in Yellow Pages for suppliers. Don't be tempted to cut corners; you will lose out in the end in terms of the time and cost involved in sorting out breakages. The packaging you use and how you pack will depend on your type of work. If your work is very fragile it may be almost impossible to ensure that it is never broken, but with care and thought most objects can be safely packed.

The first essential is that the object(s) are unable to move around in transit. If you are using newspaper as packing material, wet it first so that you can mould it around the object. Bubble-wrap works well, but polystyrene chips are not good with heavier items as the objects can work their way to the bottom. Boxes within boxes are useful for glass and ceramics; pack the object well in one box, then pack that box well within a second container. If you are packing a number of objects in one package, put light objects inside heavier ones, but never the other way round. Cushion corners with sellotape, paper, bubble-wrap, etc. and take care that they are not too close to the side of the container. For airfreighting, wooden containers are not required; toughened cardboard is acceptable. If in doubt, check with the particular airfreight company.

You must work on the assumption that all carriers drop packages frequently. If you regularly send work by carrier, make up a test consignment and drop it from height of three feet, kick it a few times and check the result.

There are sometimes restrictions on the materials used, for example, your commercial invoices for the USA may have to state that no hay or straw has been included, and newspaper is not permitted as a packing material in consignments for Saudi Arabia. Shipping agents, the DTI, the Chambers of Commerce and embassies can usually advise on any relevant restrictions.

Shipping by post

Considering the quantities likely to be involved, sending work by post is unquestionably the easiest way of getting pieces abroad. Although the limit for a single parcel is usually 10 kg, this can sometimes be increased to 20 kg. The limit for letter post is 2 kg. You will almost always find it easier and cheaper to send several parcels by post, rather than one large consignment by other methods. You can insure parcels, usually to a limit of £600, and sometimes even send them COD. Customs procedures are simplified, and a postal receipt acts as your proof of export if you are registered for VAT or need to re-import the work.

Even for a single occasion, it is worth buying the Post Office Guide, available at any main Post Office. It gives all the packing and sealing specifications, details about permitted sizes and weights, customs procedures, together with services such as insurance and cash on delivery. Information is given on each country and its customs requirements, as well as the prohibitions and restrictions on items sent by post. You can therefore see at a glance that the German Democratic Republic prohibits the sending of carrier pigeons, but will accept used textiles provided they have been cleaned and "are in an hygienically unimpeachable condition"!

If you send work by post regularly, you can get special multipart forms with all the necessary customs and record copies you need from companies such as Sitpro or Postabroad (see page 86). Otherwise consult the Guide and ask for the forms you need at the Post Office. It will save time when posting work to use main post offices.

Shipping agents and procedures

Whatever method of shipping you use, you can handle it all yourself. But if you are sending work other than by post, even if you are taking it yourself, the paperwork can be time-consuming and occasionally complex. Certainly on the first occasion it will seem complex! If you are not clear about the procedures, get help. International shipping is a very specialised activity and you will find the services of an expert are worth the fee.

The forms you require and the circumstances in which they are used vary with the work, the country to which it is going, the method of shipping, and often with the value of the consignment. Little documentation is required to ship work out of this country. It is principally needed by Customs for our export statistics. (Yes, you are making a contribution to the balance of payments!) However, you may need proof that you have exported work. In the absence of export documents giving such proof, VAT can be charge on re-imported work. Whether you are registered for VAT or not makes no difference and few things are more galling than paying tax to get your own work back into the country.

Other than by post, the cheapest method of shipping work is consolidated with other consignments travelling by road. This option is largely limited to Europe, although there are services going further afield. Many shippers run scheduled services. A little investigation will identify carriers going to , or near, your required destination. Shippers can always use local carriers to make the final delivery if it is not on their normal route. Carriers are listed in the telephone book and will tell you where they go: remember they need the size and weight of your consignment to give you a quote. You must be well organised enough to fit in with their timings for scheduled services – they are not going to wait for you.

Carriage by air is easily organised. It has the advantage of avoiding transit procedures, so that a flight from London to Rome is considered a direct British-Italian frontier crossing. Customs and cargo procedures at all major airports are computerised and the airwaybill used for air cargo is most comprehensive, covering shipping costs, insurance charges and other details. As a document of carriage it is the proof that your work has been exported, and is often used as evidence that payment is due for what has been supplied. Do not confuse air cargo with the baggage which you take yourself on a plane. The procedures are not the same. Airline staff will usually help with the paperwork for air cargo, although not the packing, provided that you have got the necessary additional documents. Air freight is charged either by weight or by volume, whichever is the larger. To allow for a very large but light consignment, the carriers will use a formula to calculate a nominal "weight by volume". If it is larger than the actual weight, it is on the nominal weight that you will be charged. You can get information of flights and a quote for the cost of air freight by ringing any appropriate airline cargo office.

Unaccompanied carriage of goods by sea is potentially the most complex and certainly the slowest method. Unless you have exceptionally heavy or large objects, or a very large quantity of work, the time taken to send goods by sea, plus the necessary trans-shipment via other types of transport to and from the ports, means that you can almost certainly find quicker and simpler methods of shipping. Cargo has to be entered on the ship's bill of landing, which like the deeds to a house, is one of the few documents still considered a document of title: the holder of a bill of landing owns the goods. Additional paperwork may be necessary to cover payment and clarify the point at which the consignment becomes the purchaser's property, and you should probably ask a shipping office to help with this paperwork.

Goods in a vehicle not unloaded on a ship on short trips (such as channel ferries) are not considered to be travelling by sea, but by the Ro-Ro (roll-on, roll-off) method. The paperwork is less complicated and probably what you require if you are taking work to Europe yourself.

For each method, whether you are using an agent or handling the shipping yourself, the basic documents are the same. It is probably a good idea to use an agent on the first occasion at least. It will give you the confidence to appreciate that shipping is not as difficult as it may seem.

Any shipping agent or international carriers can organise your shipping and handle the necessary documentation, but it is worth considering those specialising in the shipment of antiques and works of art (see page 86). Shipping is a very competitive business, so ask for several quotes.

Taking it yourself

You may find it easier and a great deal more interesting to deliver the work yourself. However you travel, once again, allow plenty of time to complete procedures even if your documents are correct. Unlike private travellers, you are shipping cargo and if you arrive at a ferry with minutes to spare you may well find a long queue of lorry drivers getting their papers stamped in front of you. Keep your journey simple, crossing as few borders as possible. If you are going to Germany, for example, it is worth sailing direct from an east coast port rather than via France, Belgium and Holland, each of whose transit procedures you would need to follow. You could arrive at the German border only to be sent back to the Franco-Belgian frontier, or even the

Channel port, to get your papers in the correct sequence. Before setting out, investigate the documents you will need. If you are not using a shipping agent to prepare them, the Chambers of Commerce will often be able to give advice. If you ask Customs and Excise, it is best to approach their offices at the port or airport from which you intend to travel. It is unwise to expect British Customs to know other countries' regulations; ask the Customs where you are going what they require. You can contact their Embassy in London or consulates around the country if necessary.

The principal document you will require is a **commercial invoice**. This is a comprehensive list of everything taken (or sent), if possible typed on your headed paper. You will need at least three copies It should be headed "Commercial Invoice" and show your name and address as supplier and the name and address of where the consignment is going. All work must be described in sufficient detail for it to be easily identified, with the number sent if multiples and their unit cost, the materials used and possibly also sizes and making techniques involved. The wholesale value of the work must be shown (not the final selling price). If you are referring to an FOB or C & F order, you must show the quoted price including transport costs. It is on this figure that any tax or duty payable will be calculated. You cannot simply list "six works of art", you must describe each piece, giving its title if appropriate and the date made. You can then add a declaration that the listed items are "original works of art", although some countries will require additional information before accepting them as such. Finally the invoice must be signed with an original, not photocopied, signature.

The commercial invoice may also have to include supplementary information, such as statements regarding the type of packing or that the goods meet necessary safety standards. You should number it as other documents may need to refer to it. Together with the document of carriage (for example, the airwaybill), it guarantees what you as exporter have sent and the price you should be paid.

If you are travelling within the EEC, you will also require a "T" form. There are different types, but you will almost certainly need Form T2L. This guarantees duty (but not VAT)-free entry into EEC countries. Since EEC procedures are standardised, Customs in this country should be able to supply the correct form and help you to complete it properly.

If you are going to Austria, Finland, Norway, Iceland, Portugal, Sweden or Switzerland (EFTA countries), the European Free Trade Agreement with EEC countries means that your work should be duty-free. In addition to your invoices, you will require a Form EUR1 if the work is valued over £3140 (1989/90 figure) or EUR2 if less. (These forms are also required for postal consignments to these countries).

If your work is going to an exhibition or trade fair and will *definitely* be returning, you use an **ATA Carnet**. No invoices are required and the document gives duty- and tax-free passage across all frontiers. It needs no other paperwork or shipping agents (although you can delegate its use to them) and once issued incurs no additional costs. It is simple to use but does take time to prepare. Carnets are issued by Chambers of Commerce and currently cost about £70, less if you are the member of a Chamber. The Carnet requires a guarantee from your bank that tax and duty up to the maximum sum liable will be paid if you do not bring all the work back. Naturally the bank will charge you for giving that guarantee, although the amount will depend upon the value of the goods. Like the commercial invoice, the Carnet is a detailed list of everything being shipped, with weights and values. A copy of the list is proved for each frontier crossed. The simplest Carnet therefore requires four copies – out of and back into this country and into and out of the other. A copy is removed at each frontier and when the consignment returns the Carnet is cancelled by the issuing Chamber of Commerce and the bank withdraws its guarantee. Remember that you cannot vary the procedure and decide to sell some of the work abroad. If you default on the terms of the Carnet, the procedures operate automatically and duty in full will be paid against your bank guarantee. You could be faced with other charges, and a lengthy and potentially expensive process to cancel the Carnet and any balance of the guarantee. However, if you are sure work will be returning the ATA Carnet is much the easiest method to use.

If you are taking a van with goods, you may be able to clear Customs at your final destination. It will be necessary for the vehicle to be closed with an official seal (either at a Customs office at the port of departure or at a major city) but means you can make a "transit clearance" through the frontier customs where delays tend to be longest. If you are travelling to a major trade fair or exhibition you may also find that they have arranged temporary customs facilities at the site.

Be careful if your documents do not have a specific destination for your work. You may have loaded the car for a general selling trip, but this can cause extra problems. In Germany such "itinerant selling" requires a permit and in other European countries you will be considered a commercial traveller. You may therefore have to consider restrictions which apply to sales in other countries. The DTI have useful booklets giving hints to exporters for most applicable countries and detailed information about itinerant selling. If you are taking pieces speculatively or on a sale-or-return basis, you may be faced with some unexpected charges. You will be importing the work into another country and within the EEC you will have to pay the VAT when clearing customs but procedures vary. In some countries you can make a temporary importation, for example, in Holland or France you may import the work, usually with the assistance of an agent, without paying tax; this would be paid on the sold items only when you bring the unsold pieces back. However, in Germany tax must be paid in full on entry and claimed back on the unsold pieces when you return. Other unexpected costs can include the ferry. Since you have goods for export entered in the ship's cargo papers, even if in a private car, you will almost certainly be charged at commercial rates for your vehicle.

Typical paperwork for a single consignment, whether taken by yourself or sent by a shipping agent, will therefore be:
a commercial invoice
a document of carriage (e.g. airwaybill)
certificate of origin or value – if required
Customs and Excise declarations if required (e.g. "T" form within the EEC)

USEFUL ADDRESSES

Department of Trade & Industry
1 Victoria Street
London SW1H 0ET
01-215 7877
(regional offices in Birmingham, Bristol, Leeds, Manchester, Newcastle-upon-Tyne, Nottingham, Cardiff, Glasgow and Belfast)

Customs and Excise
Offices throughout the country. Check the telephone directory.
Head office: Kings Beam House
Mark Lane
London EC3
01-626 1515

Export Buying Offices Association
01-493 8141
c/o Portman Ltd
360 Oxford Street
London W1A 4BX
Advice on overseas markets and paperwork.

Postal Export Documentation Sets are available from:

"Postabroad"
Formecon Services Ltd
Douglas House
Gateway
Crewe CW1 1YN
0270 587811

"Sitpro Post Packs"
Sitpro
Almack House
26-28 King Street
London SW1Y 6QW
01-214 3399

Shipping agents and carriers

See under "Shipping and forwarding agents" in Yellow Pages. Those regularly handling antiques and works of art include:

James Bourlet & Sons Ltd
3 Space Waye
Pier Road
Feltham
Middlesex TW14 0TY
01-751 1155

Pitt & Scott Ltd
20 Eden Grove
London N7
01-607 7321

T. Rogers & Co Ltd
1A Broughton Street
London SW8
01-622 6776

Wingate & Johnston Ltd
78 The Broadway
London E15
01-555 8123

Cander & White
14 Masons Yard
Duke St
London
SW1Y 6BU
01-930 5383

Atlas Air
Atlas House
Central Way
Feltham
TW14 0UV
01-890 3644
(door to door delivery)

PUBLICITY

It is fair to assume that most craftspeople want the public to know about their work; publicity is the key to bringing this about, and is an important element in the selling process. As craftwork is essentially about a person making things, it is not often possible to publicise the work without also promoting the maker. Some people dislike this personality cult, but it is important to recognise that there is great public interest in craftspeople – how they live and how they work – and the media will often insist on covering you as well as your work.

There are two types of publicity; ongoing publicity, which is keeping you and your work in the public eye, and specific publicity, such as an exhibition, open workshop or launch of a new range of work. This chapter concentrates on ongoing publicity but most of what is said is relevant to all your publicity. Publicity directly related to exhibitions is dealt with in the next chapter and by reading both chapters you should be able to work out how best to publicise any specific event. Given that it is often easier to attract publicity for something specific, it is well worth trying to present your ongoing work as though it were special; for example, you may make eggcups all the year round, but by presenting them as a special Easter range seasonal interest could bring press coverage.

The first step is to decide how much time and money you are going to spend on publicity and promotion. It is such an important aspect of your work that you should allocate a fixed percentage of your annual overheads; if you do not promote your work, it will be more difficult to sell. By allowing a fixed percentage, your promotional budget will increase as sales increase. The hope is that a little publicity at the start (when you do not have much cash available) will help your work sell a little better and therefore allow a bit more cash for publicity, leading to even better sales.

Other chapters in this book deal with promotional aids such as exhibitions and trade fairs, so this chapter will restrict itself to the use of the media for promoting your work. There are basically two types of media publicity: editorial coverage and paid advertising. Even if you only have a little cash, there is certain basic promotional material which you must have before you can start seeking press coverage. This basic material is also necessary for other business purposes so investing in it is essential.

PROMOTIONAL MATERIAL

Business card

This is basically a printed card with your name, address and telephone number, which can be given to all contacts. Your business card should reflect your work to some extent, and you should therefore make sure that it is well designed and professionally printed. If you are skilful at design and the preparation of artwork, the only cost will be having it printed. If you do not have these skills, then employ a graphic designer.

Photographs

The importance of good-quality photographs of your work is empasised throughout this book. In the case of the press, your photographs will be competing for limited space alongside professionally taken pictures, so poor photographs are just a waste of time and money. Both black-and-white prints and 35mm colour slides are needed for press and other promotion (see below).

Headed notepaper

Headed notepaper is extremely useful as the basis for all your paperwork. Well-designed headed paper is also valuable when you approach the press as it emphasises your professionalism and the quality of your work. It is sensible for the design of your notepaper and business card to be complimentary.

C.V.

A printed C.V. costs very little but a well-typed sheet of paper which is then photocopied will suffice. A curriculum vitae should include your name, address and telephone number; college/workshop training; relevant grants/awards/prizes; exhibitions of your work; and public/private collections which own your work.

These are the four basics but there is other promotional material that is invaluable; if you can afford a bit more money, you should consider investing in some or all of the following:

Postcard

Many small printers specialise in reproducing a colour photograph as a postcard; the cost is about £100 to £150 per 1,000 cards. One side of the card shows a colour photograph of a piece of your work, the other side can be left blank or have extra information printed on it. This might be information on the work, your c.v., a map of how to get to your workshop, an invitation to an exhibition, or even your Christmas card. You can sometimes arrange to have some cards printed with information and the rest left blank. The more cards you have printed, the less the cost, so it is worth considering having extra blank cards printed for later use if you are having a card printed for a private view. To find suitable postcard printers, look in *Artist's Newsletter* or *The Stage* (the weekly theatrical paper) or ask the Crafts Council.

All that you require for a postcard is a good 35mm colour slide and a typed sheet with whatever information you want on the back. (In most cases the printers will typeset this for you.) Should the resulting cards be badly printed or the image fuzzy or the wrong colours, then do not hesitate to complain and refuse to pay or demand your money back unless they are reprinted to your satisfaction.

Brochure or leaflet

While few craftspeople are in the position to afford the expensive advertising material produced by large companies, recent advances in the printing industry mean that good-quality monochrome and colour printing is now widely available at lower prices than in the past, so it may be worth investigating having a leaflet or brochure printed. If you do, make sure that they are well designed and that you know in advance how you plan to use them. If you intend to give them to shops which sell your work, remember not to put your address on the printed material as otherwise the shop will probably refuse to give them out in case customers start buying from you direct.

Poster

A poster is probably only relevant if you sell direct and want to attract people to your workshop or if you are advertising a specific event such as an exhibition.

Photocopies of previous publicity

You should keep a portfolio of any press coverage you receive, and in certain circumstances good copies of press articles can be well worth sending out to prospective clients. Note on each the name of the publication and the date the article appeared before you have the copies made. If the article is in colour, then consider having it photocopied in colour.

EDITORIAL COVERAGE

Editorial coverage in a serious newspaper or magazine will bring results that would cost thousands of pounds to achieve through purchased advertising, but it is normally only achieved after considerable outlay in promotional material, energy, research and persistence.

Researching your approach

Having organised your promotional material, you must then consider whom to approach. Craftspeople have a strong case for inclusion in local newspapers and magazines, and Features Editors may be responsive to a story about you and your work if you present them with interesting material. On a national level, it is best to approach specialist craft and design magazines which already cover work similar or relevant to your own. Try looking through different magazines to see if they carry articles on the crafts or craftspeople, or if you might be able to come up with an approach that will interest them. More and more magazines are interested in the crafts, from *Brides* to *The Face*. Time spent on research can lead to you finding unusual but valuable coverage. Foreign magazines can also be well worth contacting.

How you approach a publication will to some extent depend on what type of coverage you hope to get, so have a strong, clear idea of what it is you do want. It is worth drawing up a detailed list of the coverage you are chasing together with the names of the the people you decide to contact. Remember that magazines will want to fit you into the existing structure of their regular features: for example, "Country Matters" in *Vogue* covers rural makers, "Antennae" in *Interiors* covers new products with a strong design content, and the Women's Page of the *Daily Telegraph* regularly spotlights individual craftspeople.

Who to contact

It is very important to direct your press information to the correct person, and this means compiling a personal press list. Your own research into magazines and newspapers will give you important information for this list. You can also get valuable advice by asking friends, craft shop owners, gallery directors, regional arts press officers, officers of guilds or other craft bodies and the Crafts Council for names of relevant journalists who handle particular features or welcome craft information.

Journalists move around frequently, so it is unwise to simply "lift" a press list from someone else as it may be out of date. You can check it by consulting press directories, such as the one published by PIMS, which give comprehensive lists of publications together with the names of specialist journalists.

It is helpful to put your press list onto a card index. You will then be able to revise it easily and also make notes on the individual cards about contacts you have made with particular journalists, their likes and dislikes, freelance activities, long-term plans for articles and other information for future reference. If you are having difficulty finding a particular contact, try ringing up the publication and asking the receptionist who would be the best person to approach; if all else fails, address the letter to the "Listings Editor". "Features Editor", "Arts Reviewer" or whatever title seems relevant.

Some media coverage results from approaches made by the press to a body such as the Crafts Council or a regional arts association, so it is vital to keep such organisations supplied with up-to-date photographs, slides and information so that they may act on your behalf if they receive a media approach relevant to your work. Often press deadlines mean that there is no time for them to contact you, and the opportunity will go to those whose material is instantly available.

Timing your approach

Most people get caught out in their first attempts at publicity by the length of time newspapers, magazines and radio and television programmes need to plan ahead. Magazines which print in colour usually work *at least* three months ahead; this means that ideally you should contact them four months in advance, and be able to supply colour transparencies and detailed information fairly soon afterwards. This often creates problems, for example, when work for an exhibition is still being made and details of the event are not finalised. But if you want the publicity, you will have to find a way around this, perhaps by supplying photos of existing work similar to the pieces in the exhibition, and taking calculated risks in predicting what can safely be said about the arrangements.

If you are negotiating for a major feature, it is important that you start talking to the magazine as early as possible as the basic contents of an issue will be planned as much as a year ahead. Bear in mind that most magazines start thinking about their Christmas features in July, and that you will always stand a better chance with an idea which is related to the seasonal emphasis of the particular magazine. For example, approach fashion writers about sweaters in May for publication in September when they start covering winter clothes. If you are simply hoping to be included in a regular feature, such as *Observer* "Billboard", *Vogue* "Notices" or *Interiors* "Exhibition Diary", the most important thing is to supply a good photograph and clear, accurate, basic information to the correct person in good time.

Magazines which print in black and white usually go to press about six weeks before they appear. Again, features are planned further ahead, so you should discuss this type of coverage with the magazine well in advance. Regular items, such as listings and notebook columns, are usually compiled as close as possible to the press date from whatever material has come into the office – make sure yours is there.

Newspapers are the most flexible and responsive section of the press. For a major feature or article, it is best to approach the relevant journalist about one month in advance. With more straightforward coverage, such as listings, reviews and news items, you need to approach the paper about ten days before the event – too early and they're likely to lose or forget about your material; too late may mean they've already planned to include something else.

Radio can be an important medium for promoting visual work; even though there are no pictures, it can help attract people to your workshop or an event, and get your name more widely known. The development of local radio has greatly increased access to radio broadcasting, and your local radio station may be worth considering in any publicity campaign. Most radio stations run a number of magazine programmes which cover events of a local nature. Research the names and format of all suitable programmes and approach them individually with the relevant information about two weeks before the event. They are likely to put your material into a "planner" diary for consideration a few days before broadcast date, so it is a good idea to follow up your initial approach with a telephone call to check that they have the information and to find out whether any coverage is being considered.

National radio operates in the same way, although only events of truly national interest stand a chance of achieving coverage. Don't waste time sending information to national radio stations unless you are convinced that you have a unique and particularly interesting story to offer.

Local television operates in a similar way to local radio, although there is likely to be less airtime available as they also broadcast a large amount of national networked programmes. Research the local magazine programmes which often go out around tea-time either side of the six o'clock news, and also the local news slot which will sometimes consider carrying an "art" item if it has a sufficiently interesting storyline. Local television stations also run their own arts programmes, although these tend to be seasonal. You need to carry out a fair amount of research to discover which are the relevant programmes, when their broadcast seasons start and finish, who to approach and to do this in sufficient time for your work to be considered.

National television is probably the hardest kind of coverage to achieve: it includes only a small amount of arts broadcasting which is planned far in advance, and arts material has to compete with every other kind of item for inclusion in news and magazine broadcasts. This results in very limited coverage, often of either a sensational or a trivial nature. Timing your approach to television is similar to radio; two weeks in advance is sufficient for a magazine item, but major coverage should be set in motion as early as possible so that the item can be considered as part of the overall planning of a series.

CONTACTING THE PRESS

As with everyone you send information to, whatever you send will be competing with a mass of other information so try to think of imaginative ways to make yours stand out. Aim to send something which a journalist will pin on the notice board instead of just tossing it into the wastepaper basket.

When you contact the press you should send a letter, a press release, photographs/slides or a combination of these.

By letter

Be concise but interesting. If you have written to the journalist because of an article you have read, it may be worth mentioning your appreciation of it. Explain why you think you and your work are of interest. Attach a photograph of a piece of work and any other relevant information, but do not send too much. Follow up your letter with a telephone call after a week or so, but if you get a cool reception leave it at that.

Press release

This may sound like a glamorous and mysterious document; in fact, it is only a piece of paper containing concise information relevant to the press.

A press release should cover what, where, why, when, not necessarily in that order. It should start with an eye-catching and interesting first sentence, which will give the recipient an incentive to read on. Sometimes it is possible to give a press release a short title which sums up the general message in the style of a journalistic headline, but take care not to be over-clever.

Remember that journalists are very busy, constantly working under pressure, so they are looking for news or interesting stories. They are unlikely to be interested in details of your aesthetic decisions, although they may well like to know that you have invented a new technique, constructed the largest coiled pot or been commissioned by a famous person. This apparently trivial approach does not mean that the press are a bad lot; it reflects the fact that they have to persuade their editors to run arts stories against competing claims from sport, gossip, scandal and the crime desk, and that the management's overall concern is to sell newspapers. The technique to adopt at press release stage is to get the journalist interested and encourage him or her to follow up whatever you are promoting, at which stage it will be possible to introduce the writer or broadcaster to the work and take the whole business onto a more serious level.

Press releases should be as short as possible; only the most exceptionally complex exhibition requires more than one side of A4, and it is usually possible to say all that needs saying in three or four short paragraphs. The layout of the press release can also contribute to its effectiveness. You are promoting visual goods, so the choice of paper, the typeface, width of margin and use of colour should all echo your own high standards, as well as presenting the message in a clear and attractive manner.

You may wish to include some visual reference about the work; some photographs will photocopy effectively and can be used either on the press release itself, or on an attached sheet. If you have a postcard of a piece of work this would be a useful enclosure. It is not necessary, or expected to send out unsolicited press photographs at press release stage.

Every press release should have a "nuts and bolts" section which includes the relevant items from the following list:
dates, place and opening times of any event
admission charges, if any
availability of press photographs, b/w and/or colour
availability of work for viewing
availability of work for photography
press preview arrangements
availability of catalogue; whether or not it is illustrated, number of pages, price, cost of p & p
telephone number and name of person to contact for further information

It is difficult to be objective enough about your own work to write an effective press release, so consider asking someone else to write it.

Press photographs

Newspapers or magazines which print in black and white require high quality, high-contrast black and white photographs, which are normally printed on 10in × 8in paper. Bear in mind that any photographs you supply will be competing with a lot of other images on the editor's desk.

The press do not expect to have photographs suppied automatically with a press release. However, journalists do expect a good selection of pictures to be available to them immediately upon request – it is not good enough to say that your brother-in-law is coming round with his Nikon in ten days' time!

Photographs should always carry a caption, in the form of a typed label attached to the back of the picture, giving details of what is shown in the photo and the photographer's name if he/she should be credited.

Example of caption:
Jane Jones completing work on her slate-cut plaque, to be unveiled by HRH The Princess of Wales when she opens Middletown Children's Hospital on Tuesday 14 February

Photo credit: Jim Smith

Please return to Jane Jones, The Old Schoolhouse, Middletown

It is not wise to count on photographs being returned after use; order a good supply in the first instance, regard them as gone, and those which do come back will be a useful bonus. Make sure that any photographs which have to be sent by post are packed between sheets of stiff cardboard, or in card-backed envelopes. The press cannot reproduce from a black and white photograph which has already been printed, for instance in a catalogue, but require an original print.

Colour photographs in magazines and catalogues are taken from colour slides or transparancies, *not* prints. It is important to try to supply originals, not copy slides, so take, or ask the photographer to take, multiple exposures to give you an adequate supply. 35mm slides give a good quality reproduction and are adequate for most situations. Sometimes large-format transparancies (5in × 4in or larger) are used where particularly high quality is required. Slides should be captioned in the same way as black and white photos. It is a good idea to pack slides in transparent plastic wallets with rows of pockets, available from photographic shops, with the captions typed on labels affixed to the relevant pockets. Put a number on each slide and a matching number on each caption. Always pack slides carefully for posting, particularly if they are mounted between glass.

It is important to be sure that you are not infringing anyone's copyright when you supply photographs to the press, because you imply that you are in a position to grant the right to reproduce them. As a general rule, if you commission photographs it is a good idea to state, in writing, at the start of the transaction that you wish to buy the copyright.

Checking copy

Makers are understandably concerned whether they will have the opportunity to correct copy which is written about them before it is printed. There is no general rule about this; some journalists like to check copy in advance, and others simply do not operate in this way. A sensible compromise is to ask whether you will have the opportunity to check copy, make it as easy as possible for the journalist to reach you, but don't alienate someone who is in a position to help you by making a fuss if it becomes clear that he or she cannot give you advance access to the material.

PAID ADVERTISING

Buying advertising space is another way of achieving communication with the readership of a particular publication. All the available research on effective publicity indicates that people respond to a broad range of promotional activity, and an effective campaign will include several different elements which link up with each other to convey an overall message. Few craftspeople or crafts organisations are likely ever to be in a financial position to consider promoting their work through advertising as a primary medium; however, it can have an important role to play in conjunction with other publicity activity.

Classified advertising

This is an inexpensive form of advertising where a newspaper or publication groups announcements of a similar nature together under a generic heading; craftspeople are most likely to be concerned with classified categories for the promotion of exhibitions, ongoing promotion of a workshop sales outlet, a service or a particular object. Because classified advertising is inexpensive it can only convey basic information – times, places, dates, names. It relies on other media to persuade the audience of the interest and value of the facility on offer.

Display advertising

This is the term used for advertisements which appear within marked-out panels, individually designed, and either grouped together with other advertisements or interspersed in the text of newspapers or magazines. The cost of advertising is given on the magazine's rate card, supplied on request; major publications list their rates in the directory *British Rates and Data* (BRAD). Rates for display advertisements vary enormously, and you should find out how many copies the particular publication sells in order to evaluate its effectiveness as an advertising medium. Some small magazines quote you the number of copies which they *print* rather than the number which they *sell*, unless correctly questioned, and a smart advertising manager will always tell you the estimated readership, usually much greater than the number of copies distributed on the basis that more than one person will read each copy.

You can compare the advertising value offered by different publications if you divide the cost of the advertising space by the number of people reached.

Directory entries

It is worth keeping an eye on directories, yearbooks and handbooks, particularly if you are trying to promote a particular type of work to a professional group, for example wallhangings to architects. Some directories carry basic entries free, but charge for a fuller listing – read the sales literature carefully. It is unwise to spend money on advertising in a new publication of this type; wait until it has proved itself, and become a known and trusted reference work.

Arranging advertising

Having decided which publications you will advertise with, find out the copy date for the particular issue in which you want to appear. You will then have to prepare the artwork from which the advertisements will be printed. Most art magazines, and many general interest magazines, will design and make up advertisement artwork for a small extra charge. This will be in a compatible style to the rest of the magazine and of professional appearance, but you must not expect to be able to stipulate more than a very general description of how you wish the advertisement to look.

If you want to have greater artistic control over the appearance of your advertisement, you will need to commission a graphic designer or prepare the artwork yourself if you have the necessary experience. But remember that large unionised magazines and newspapers will not carry artwork prepared by non-union designers. You will need a separate piece of artwork for every publication in which you have booked space; it is not realistic to expect to transfer artwork from one publication to another. Artwork should be prepared wherever possible to the exact size of the advertisement space; this is known as "s/s" artwork. If the printers have to enlarge, reduce or carry out any other technical work on your artwork, they will charge extra.

When the advertisement appears, the publisher should send you a copy of the magazine or newspaper, with the bill. This is known as supplying a "voucher copy". These copies are sent out as soon as the publication appears, so that advertisers cannot claim the publication did not occur on time. If you book an advertisement which appears after the event has taken place because the magazine came out late, you are entitled to ask for a reduction as long as the expected publication date was clearly established as part of the original contract between you and the publisher.

You may wish to use advertising to invite people to send for your brochure, arrange a visit to your workshop, etc. You can assess the effectiveness of your advertising by monitoring the replies. If you are advertising in several publications, you could consider using different names (J. Jones, Jones Knitwear, JJ Knits, Jonwear Knits), thus enabling you to assess the number, type and quality of replies attracted by each which will guide you when placing future advertisements.

PUBLIC RELATIONS

PR is a separate area of activity to advertising and publicity, but so closely related that it is necessary to make some comment about its influence. In the simplest terms, PR is your relationship with the outside world. Publicity gobbles up time and money; good PR means that *in addition* you take the trouble to do things over and above the minimum standard required, exhibiting good grace, energy and enterprise.

Examples of good PR are bothering to make a special journey to deliver press photos at the end of a long day, cancelling a visit to your mother because a writer cannot interview you at any other time, and being cheerful when someone rings up to check details on a piece at eleven o'clock at night. The demands made on you will often be unfair, unreasonable and unrealistic, but if you are readily available, willing and helpful, publicity opportunities will come your way more and more frequently.

EXHIBITING

"How do I arrange to have an exhibition of my work?" is a question craftspeople often ask. We will concentrate here on exhibitions which involve a large body of one person's work, either individually or as part of a group show, rather than mixed exhibitions which include a few pieces by a great number of different craftspeople. This is not to belittle such exhibitions; they are important but are not normally organised by individual craftsmen and women.

The easiest way to have an exhibition of your own is to be asked to do so by an established gallery or shop. Of course, this very rarely comes out of the blue and you will usually need to spend time building up contacts and approaching possible galleries about exhibiting your work. To those fortunate enough to be invited to exhibit, check carefully what the gallery will provide. You should expect the gallery to pay for transport of the work, insurance, publicity, the catalogue and the private view. However, you should also expect them to take a sizeable commission on sales in return for their promotion of you and your work. Unfortunately we do not live in a perfect world, and in some cases you may discover that the gallery expects you to contribute towards all or part of the exhibition costs. So take care that you are clear about who pays for what when making an agreement.

If you are expected to contribute, then you will have to balance the cost against the possible advantages and decide whether it is worth going ahead. Furthermore, if you have to contribute to the costs, you should expect the gallery to charge less commission on sales.

For those who have not been approached by galleries in this way, the alternative is to do it yourself. However, do consider whether the time spent organising your own show might not be better used in pursuing the contacts which could lead to an established gallery inviting you to exhibit. If you do decide to do it yourself, note that, as with all DIY, unless care is taken there is a danger of hitting your own thumb.

EXHIBITION VENUES

What is the primary purpose of organising your own show? Is it to sell your work, to gain general publicity, to interest people in commissioning work from you, for prestige, or merely to add a useful line to your c.v.? In most cases, of course, an exhibition will involve more than one of these purposes but you should decide the primary reason in order to choose what type of venue to go for.

If you are content to have a small show involving a few selected objects, then it may be worth exploring the possibility of using building society or bank windows in your area. Such organisations often make their windows available free of charge. A few objects interestingly displayed, combined with well-laid-out information about your work (including prices), where it can be bought and a contact address, can be a relatively cheap way to promote your work. Another possibility is to see if your local library has one or two display cases which you could use for a small show. An extension of this idea might be to fix up a number of different venues and arrange a small tour of the show. For example, two weeks in four different venues would increase the number of people seeing your work for minimal effort.

If you wish your exhibition to be more than a small selection of objects, one useful area to explore is local authority galleries. Many of these receive no additional funds to mount exhibitions, so the people in charge may be glad of the chance to show some craftwork at no cost to the gallery. Some may charge, some may just provide free space, while others may offer space plus other facilities. In addition to local authority galleries, it is also worth investigating those attached to a local educational establishment. Other possibilities include small private galleries, which can often be hired, and the foyer spaces of public buildings such as libraries, theatres and concert halls. In choosing a space, remember to take into account the facilities available, such as lighting, display cases (important where these are essential for the security of your work), public accessibility etc. and to balance these against any cost of hiring. A useful publication for help in finding an exhibition venue is *Directory of Exhibition Spaces*, available from Artic Producers, P.O. Box 23, Old Simpson Street School, Simpson Street, Sunderland SR4 6DG, price £12.50.

Having chosen the venue, you need to decide whether the exhibition should be of your work alone or whether it should involve a number of others. This choice will be based partially on preference and partially on circumtances. You know your own preference; what about circumstances? The main point to take into account is the certain saving in time and money gained by sharing an exhibition. But savings will only come about if those joining together in the exhibition carefully divide the cost and workload before beginning the arrangement. In dividing the workload, take care to allocate tasks to those most suited to carry them out. There is little point in making the shyest member responsible for press contact, or in giving charge of the finances to the person whose workshop drawer is renowned for its collection of unpaid, coffee-stained invoices, crumpled tax demands and assorted recipes for glazes.

BUDGET

Before deciding whether to organise an exhibition, you will need to assess if you can afford to do this, be it by yourself or sharing with others. First you should list the areas of likely expenditure, and then estimate what each will cost or what you can afford.

If you are unsure of the costs, it can be helpful to talk to a gallery or to someone who has organised an exhibition before. It is also useful to get a few estimates for such costs as catalogue printing, posters, etc. The main areas of expenditure will be hire of the gallery, special display, hire of cases, insurance, transport, photography, posters, catalogue, leaflets, publicity, postage, telephone and the private view. If there is any income from the catalogue sales or fees from participants, then that will help to offset the expenditure. Once you know the likely cost, you will be able to see how feasible the exhibition is and assess whether or not it is worth going ahead.

With the venue agreed and the composition of the exhibition sorted out, the next step is to fix a date. Two points here. The first also touches upon financing the exhibition: it may be possible to obtain some grant aid towards mounting the exhibition through you regional arts association and it is worth contacting the appropriate officer to find out if the project would be eligible. If you wish to apply for a grant, remember that the funding body will need plenty of time to consider your application and that there will be some delay between applying and being advised whether your application has been successful.

The other point to remember is that organising the exhibition will take a lot of time. Do not plan the date three months ahead if it will take you three months to make the actual pieces to be exhibited, for you will find the time required for organisational details conflicts with the making. If your timescale does not adequately allow for both the making of work and the organisation of the exhibition, then postpone the date. The length of the exhibition will probably be fixed by the venue, but do ensure that it is neither so short that publicity and word of mouth have no time to take effect nor so long that it puts a burden on your time and finances. In general, two weeks is the minimum extent and one month the maximum. The length is particularly relevant if you are having to staff the show for security reasons.

WHAT NEXT?

A great deal of work and a few panics. As with most things, organising an exhibition seems relatively straightforward to those who have previous experience whereas to those attempting it for the first time it can appear a minefield. It need not be so. By talking to people who are involved in exhibition organisation, you can quickly gather the basic know-how. The Arts Council publishes a booklet entitled *Organising Exhibitions* by Teresa Gleadowe which is an extremely helpful guide to such subjects as the loan of work, insurance, transport, the catalogue, etc.

Display is crucial. There is little point in spending time creating fine objects if these are then badly displayed. A dowdy display will ruin even the best object and you must ensure that stands, display cases, etc. are fresh-looking (at the very least, clean). Display is one area where imagination and care can compensate to a great extent for a shortage of cash. Do not forget to check the display regularly throughout the period of the exhibition as grubby fingers and dust can ruin the original effect. Labelling exhibits gives a professional feel to the exhibition. Labels should be typed (unless your craft is calligraphy!) and mounted on thick card which will not curl; include the maker's name (if a group show), the date of making, details of the medium/process, the catalogue number (if any), the owner (if borrowed) and the selling price.

Given that your exhibition will be trying to attract the attention of the public and the press, it is worth considering what to call the exhibition. The title can be informative or catchy, depending on the audience you hope to attract. However, do remember that such titles as "An Exhibition of New Work by Jones and Smith" will not necessarily mean much to those who do not know what Jones and Smith make. So make sure that the title indicates what will be on show.

Insurance should be thought about, unless the gallery provides cover for your work during the exhibition. Security may also have to be considered and often this will involve being on hand to keep an eye on the exhibits.

Publicity is essential but this is an area where money and time can easily be wasted. First, consider carefully what you would like the publicity to do. Having decided that, try to direct your publicity efforts to the most suitable places. Press coverage is free publicity but in order to obtain such coverage a lot of patient effort must be expended. See the previous chapter for information on media publicity.

A poster can be useful but can also be expensive. One possibility is to combine the poster with the catalogue as a broadsheet so that the print run is extended and savings made by not having to do the two separately. Take care that the size of the poster is right for the sites where it is to be displayed: too large and some will refuse to put it up, too small and it may not be noticed by anyone. A3 or Crown is probably the right size.

Whether or not to have a catalogue will, to a great extent, be decided by the cash you have available or the friendliness of your bank manager. A catalogue is basically a list of the exhibits, although it can be expanded to become much more. One possible alternative (in addition to the idea of a combined poster/catalogue broadsheet just mentioned) is to have a brochure printed giving informaiton on you and your work which, when combined with a simple typed list of exhibits, will work as a catalogue and will also be useful after the exhibition for general promotion. Similarly, if you want to have a special private view card printed, one idea might be to have a postcard with a colour photograph on one side and private view information on the other. (For a print run of 1000 , the cost at current prices would be about £150; the more you have printed, the less the cost per card.) By extending the print run with the private view information omitted, you could provide yourself with blank postcards showing one piece of your work for little extra cost.

Remember to check that the copy for any poster, publicity leaflet, invitation card or press release includes the title of the exhibition, the venue's address, the period of exhibition, the times of opening and admission charges (if any). The date and time for the private view must also be included on the invitation card and the press release. It is essential that copy is carefully checked (several times) as a mistake on basic details can cause embarrassment and confusion. Care should also be taken to include any acknowledgements on publicity material where this is required (for example, "subsidised by the Crafts Council", "with the help of the Gresham Company"). All invitations to the private view should go out at least a fortnight before the actual date.

PRESS AND PRIVATE VIEWS

If you are holding an exhibition or special event, you may wish to hold a press view and/or a private view. This is by no means obligatory, and it is better not to do it unless you have reason to be confident that sufficient people will turn up to prevent it being an embarrassment. The reason for holding a press preview is to give journalists an opportunity to see the work in advance of the general public, and to speak to the maker(s) away from all the commotion of a normal private view.

However, few small exhibitions are likely to attract a sufficient number of journalists and it is probably more sensible to invite them to the private view, with the offer of a quiet look round beforehand. If you do decide to hold a press preview, the best time is the lunchtime preceding the opening day of the exhibition, with the private view in the evening. Check whether any other press events are taking place at the same time; it can be an advantage to overlap with a relevant event in a nearby venue, but a disaster if all the journalist are at a competing event on the other side of town. The press normally ignore RSVP requests, but if you want to have some indication of attendance in advance a separate pre-addressed reply card will produce some results. It is normal to provide wine or other drinks at a press preview and sometimes snacks or a buffet lunch. People do not write reviews as a result of a few plates of sandwiches, but providing refreshments can be a way of extending a hospitable welcome to members of the press, whose help you are hoping to receive.

Provide a visitor's book at the entrance to the gallery, and ask guests to sign as they arrive; this enables you to find out who people are. You may wish to offer complimentary catalogues and any other supporting information at this point. Display a full set of press photographs in some convenient prominent place, and put someone in charge of handing out copies of these on request. It is a good idea to make a note of those who take photographs as this will help you look out for subsequent coverage.

After the preview(s), look through the visitor's book and establish whether there are any journalists or other people you (realistically) hoped would attend and didn't. It is still possible to write or telephone to say how sorry you were that they were unable to make the preview and encourage them to visit the exhibition during the normal opening period. However, do learn to take "no" for an answer and gracefully let the matter drop if you are obviously making no headway.

It is important to find out the name and position of the journalists you wish to approach, and to spell their names correctly when you write to them.

If you are arranging a private view and wish to extend the range of people invited, it is worth asking the venue, other galleries, local art and design colleges, your regional arts association and other craft and art organisations for suggestions or lists. Do take care, however, not to duplicate invitations or to invite too many people. Other gallery and shop owners/directors can be worth inviting as they may be impressed enough to offer you a show at their gallery. Regional arts officers and Crafts Council staff should also be included. Even if none of these come to the private view, some may well come along to the exhibition later. A private view can also be a good way of thanking people who have helped – your bank manager again – and do not forget to invite friends and relations. Your Aunt Eliza may very well be the first peron to buy something and so encourage a rash of red spots.

AFTERWARDS

When the exhibition is over, send letters of thanks to anyone who has helped or lent work. Figures for attendances and catalogue sales (if known) should be recorded and copies of all publicity material carefully kept for future record. A final account of the income and expenditure relating to the exhibition is worth drawing up, and this will be essential if any grants have been received. Send a copy of the accounts and a report on the exhibition to all those who gave financial assistance.

And what will be the result of all your work and sleepless nights? All your work sold? Gallery owners clamouring to promote your next show? More commissions than you can handle? Photographs of your work in every colour magazine? Your overdraft repaid? Well, perhaps not, but hopefully some work will have sold, contacts will have been made and your work more widely seen.

HEALTH

Craft workshops can be potentially hazardous places and as you will have no income if you are injured or fall ill, you must take care to try and cut down the risks.

Too often craftspeople work with unsafe machinery which endangers both themselves and others working in or visiting the workshop. Also craftspeople are sometimes ignorant of the dangers caused by exposure to dust, fumes and harmful materials. Illnesses related to these hazards can take years to manifest themselves, so always be on the look-out for advance warning signs, such as headaches, coughs, asthma, dizziness, etc. If you often feel under the weather when you are in the workshop but better away from it, then this is a strong indication that something at work is affecting you.

Given the variety of hazards encountered in different crafts, it is not possible to do more than give some general guidance. For fuller information it is well worth obtaining a copy of *Caution: A Guide to Safe Practice in the Arts and Crafts* by Tim Challis and Gary Roberts, available from Sunderland Polytechnic Faculty of Art and Design.

THE WORKSHOP

Be aware of the fire escape routes from your workshop and ensure that these are kept unobstructed at all times. Keep a fire extinguisher in the workshop and check it regularly. Note that water extinguishers must not be used on electrical fires, or on burning oils or solvents. Your local fire station will advise on types of fire extinguishers for your activites. Check that all wiring is safe and that everything is earthed.

Keep the workshop clean and tidy, and the floor clear of anything you might trip over or slip on. You should regularly vacuum or wet-mop to keep the dust down; dry brushing will only move the dust around.

It is best not to smoke in the workshop or to eat or drink there, as this can increase the chance of accidentally ingesting hazardous materials. If you work from home, do not contaminate your living area and never use the kitchen area as a work space. It is illegal to pour toxic chemicals down the drain, and inadvisable to pour any chemicals down the drain unless safely diluted.

Always have a source of fresh air in the workshop – an open window or air intake. For many activities, additional ventilation will be essential. If you create a lot of dust, a vacuum cleaner set up next to the dust source can be helpful. For toxic materials, use a strong exhaust fan to draw harmful materials and fumes away from your face and use a spray booth for spraying glazes, paints, etc. All kilns and furnaces should be ventilated via a canopy hood or chimney, vented to the outside. Make certain that any outlet is well away from air intakes.

You need to work in sufficient light, ideally natural light with artificial lighting merely supplementing it.

PROTECTIVE CLOTHING

Dust, flying fragments or splashes of harmful materials can damage your eyes so wear goggles where necessary. Dark green spectacles need to be worn if you are working with furnaces to protect your eyes from harmful infra-red rays. It may also be necessary to protect your hands, and stout footwear can reduce the danger of injury from falling weights or spilled liquids. Keep your clothing free of dust.

EQUIPMENT AND MATERIALS

Adequate guarding of machinery is vital and certain equipment, especially wood and metal-working machinery, must be guarded by law – these guards should always be used. When you are using machinery, tie back long hair and restrain flapping clothing. Leave adequate space around machinery and check it regularly. Badly designed equipment can cause back strain and it is worth investigating this when you are purchasing it.

Kilns should be located in a separate room from your general work area with the operating instructions clearly written nearby.

Be careful with materials, even those which are labelled non-toxic, for some materials labelled thus in the past have since been shown to have harmful effects. Again, watch out for tell-tale signs. Many illnesses caused by chemicals result from a long build-up of poisons in the body and certain chemicals can combine to produce even more dangerous effects. You therefore need to know the exact identity of all the materials you are using and you should check for any toxicity. Glazes, dyes, chemicals, etc. can be potentially harmful and, given that dermatitis is common, it is essential that you take precautions. Hands and nails should be washed thoroughly after handling materials and after all work periods. Work surfaces should be kept clean and should be impervious – an untreated wooden surface will tend to retain harmful chemicals. Be especially careful if you have minor cuts and abrasions. If you use toxic materials, it is worth having your workshop regularly tested for contamination by the Health and Safety Inspector.

Keep a well-stocked first aid box handy in the workshop. If you are employing people you must record all injuries to employees in an "accident" book.

If you need any advice on specific points relating to health and safety at work, contact your local office of Health and Safety Executive. As well as offering advice and information, the Executive issues a number of useful booklets relating to specific industries and problems.

STAYING HEALTHY

Fixing some rules for hours/days worked is useful, for example, not more than ten hours in any one day (with occasional exceptions) and at least one day off every week. Stop for short rests over a cup of tea or coffee, have a decent break or short walk at lunchtime, and stop when you feel over-tired.

Watch what you eat – it is easy to eat irregularly or badly when under pressure – and what you drink – hang-overs will slow you down and, while no-one will breathalyse you while in charge of your business, alchohol can dissipate time and money.

Be careful when lifting and carrying weights. If you are working in a fixed position for a time, take short breaks to ease the muscles. Similarly, if you are working for a long period on small, concentrated details give your eyes periodic rests.

Take holidays. Even a short break can help recharge your batteries and give you renewed energy and enthusiasm.

If you do get ill, do not struggle on and make yourself worse. Better to take one day off immediately than four days off later; if you are under the weather your efficiency may be so low that you might as well be in bed.

Coping with problems

Worrying about problems can make you ill. There are bound to be points of crisis so try and learn to cope with them as best you can. Worry, depression and fatigue create a state of mind where all problems take on the same weight, so the first thing to do is to try and put your problems in perspective. Several fairly minor problems can combine and seem overwhelming, so attempt to separate them out and assess each one in turn. Making a list might help. Then tackle each problem individually and in turn.

Do not let problems drag on. It is a common failing to ignore problems in the hope that they will go away, but for every one that does nine get worse! Tackling problems quickly will nearly always make them easier to sort out and stop them niggling away at the back of your mind.

Do not hesitate to seek help or advice from relevant organisations. If you are in doubt as to whom to turn to for help you can always approach the Crafts Council – even if they cannot help directly, they will at least point you in the right direction.

Forget your problems for a while by going for a walk, visting an exhibiton or having a short break. Often you will find this gives you fresh energy to tackle things.

Finally try not to let your problems make you forget the talents and skills you possess. It may seem very easy to say "Think positively", but it is the key to coping with crisis – to succeed you must learn to balance your problems against your successes.

EXPANDING

If you are selling all or most of what you make and have a long waiting list of orders/commissions, you should perhaps be considering expanding your business. However, before deciding to purchase new equipment, employ people or move to larger premsies, you must carefully consider whether this is necessarily the best answer.

For some, it may be sufficient to raise the selling price as this can reduce demand to more manageable levels and bring in increased income. For others, where the increase in demand is merely short-term, employing some temporary help or hiring equipment may be all that is required.

To judge whether expansion is the correct step, you need to be certain that the increase in sales will compensate for the cost of expanding the business. In assessing the cost, take account of extra time spent on administration, selling, etc. as this will be time lost to actual making. Thus, the cost of employing someone, both in wages and time spent overseeing them, may be more than the income from the resulting extra work produced, in which case such a step would be unwise. On the other hand, employing someone may release you from unprofitable tasks around the workshop and allow you to spend more time making, which may lead to an increase in sales far in excess of the actual cost of the employee. Purchasing new equipment may seem expensive at the time but can be extremely profitable when the saving on your time is calculated over the next two or three years. If, on balance, expansion seems the right move, then the following points need to be considered.

FINANCE

If you are going to expand, it is likely that you will need additional cash and again it is important to use a cash flow forecast to see what additional funding you require. Undertaking more work will often mean buying larger amounts of raw materials, employing staff or sub-contracting work, purchasing new equipment and generally paying out more cash which will not be recouped until the cash from increased sales is received. You may be able to obtain a deposit/pre-payment from the customer – if it is a specific commission, this should be insisted upon – which will assist you with your cash flow.

Having prepared a cash flow forecast, you may find that the expansion can be funded out of your own savings or income from current sales. If not, then you will probably have to approach your bank for a loan or increased overdraft limit, or investigate possible grants (see chapter 1).

ADMINISTRATION

If you expand, you may also need to ensure that your administration is improved. A simple book-keeping system and a rough-and-ready way of dealing with paperwork may have been fine up till now, but expansion will usually require a more professional approach, especially as it may mean that you have to register for VAT. One answer is to employ someone to undertake this work; a professional book-keeper will do it quicker and more effectively, and release you to do what you are best at – namely, designing and making. Often someone employed for even a few hours a week is sufficient and thus the actual cost may not be very much. There are also firms which offer a comprehensive book-keeping service, including handling staff wages, VAT, tax, national insurance, etc., and a service such as this may be worth investigating if you employ a number of staff.

Micro-computers

The main use of micro-computers is for dealing with book-keeping and related paperwork. They can be used in any small business, but they are most relevant for those with large turnovers and therefore a lot of accounting and paperwork. Computers have to be "written up" just like other systems, so if you find it hard to keep your books up to date computers will not solve your basic problem. Where computers can help is by giving you flexibility with the financial information which they record. If you are considering using a micro-computer for your business, then you need to investigate the most relevant "software" package. (The term "software" simply means a computer programme.) If you are already "into" computers, then it is probably worth considering, but if computers are a strange world to you then you will need advice and guidance before investing money in one for business purposes.

Micro-computers can also be used in design and there are a growing number of uses of computers in crafts, for example, computerised knitting machines. Clearly, with the rapid developments in computers, this is something to be aware of but again you will need specialist advice.

EMPLOYING STAFF

As your business grows, you may decide to have certain objects or parts of objects which you sell made for you by someone else. This can be organised by employing staff or out-workers, or sub-contracting work to another workshop or company. Or if an object sells particularly well, you might consider having it manufactured and sold by someone else under licence.

Clearly this decision can be sensible as it allows you to produce more work, to have objects or parts produced more quickly and at less cost, or to employ skills you do not posses. However, you need to ensure that the quality of the final product is not impaired for it is this quality of making which you as a craftsperson, will be selling. If work is selling under your name, even if someone else is actually making part or all of it, you must exercise stringent quality control or your may start losing sales.

Before employing anyone to undertake work for you, check their quality of making to ensure it meets your standard. You must also be careful that outworkers or sub-contractors deliver on time – extremely important if you have contracted to produce work by a specific date as you will still be the person liable for late delivery.

If you are employing people, it is important to be aware of the requirements of the law; given the mass of employment legislation which now exists, it is worth contacting your local Employment Office for advice and information.

Costing can also become much more complicated (as though it is not complicated enough already!) when you start employing others or sub-contracting part of the making. Given that each situation will involve a variety of factors, it is impossible to lay down guidelines and it may be best to seek advice if you are uncertain how to recost your work. Again, remember that extra administration – more detailed book-keeping, dealing with staff, expanded paperwork, etc. – can reduce the time spent actually making and designing, and you have to take care that a proper balance is arrived at to ensure that you still enjoy your business.

Sub-contracting

Sometimes due to lack of equipment or skill, it may be necessary to have part of an object made by someone else, or you may find that a regular component can be produced more quickly and/or cheaper by another manufacturer. In such cases you may consider sub-contracting work although, as emphasised previously, you must be confident that the sub-contractor can work to a sufficient standard and keep to agreed schedules. In sub-contracting work you are making a contract for services – see the legal point in the section on employing outworkers.

Selling under licence

Basically this is a process whereby you give someone the right to make and sell one of your designs in exchange for a fee and/or royalty. Given that most craft objects sell because they are individually made, this option will seldom be relevant, but it is worth considering where one of your objects is in great demand and could be mass-produced or produced on a limited basis by another manufacturer. The Chartered Society of Designers (address Page 74) publish guides to royalty agreements, etc.

Outworkers/freelancers/casual help

There is a widespread but mistaken belief that by using outworkers or casual help no employer/employee relationship exists. The reality is that if they expect to be given detailed instruction about what to do and how to do it then you are employing them. On the other hand there is no contract of employment, only a contract for services, if
(a) you have no control over their method of working, for example, when you employ a plumber to repair a drain, where you will not be directing how he/she goes about it; or
(b) the person undertaking the work is not bound to carry out the work him/herself, for example, when you contract a company or individual to supply goods (even if to your design) but they then employ someone else to carry out the work.
Thus if you pay outworkers to make work (as many knitters do) or someone to help you out in your workshop, you will be employing them whether payment is by a lump sum, a weekly wage, an hourly rate or for each piece produced. This is an important point because, while no contract of employment need be issued, there are legal requirements covering tax and National Insurance (see page 120) and people employed regularly as outworkers or freelancers can be covered by other employment legislation.

While the tax and NI requirements are explicit, many employers and casual outworkers are ignorant of or confused about them. Much of this confusion is encouraged by individuals who are knowingly evading tax, but be warned that to connive, knowingly or through ignorance, in such tax evasion can lead to trouble. The Inland Revenue is cracking down on this form of tax evasion and if it is discovered that you have been employing people without deducting and paying tax then you can be charged with all the tax that should have been paid.

You may find that when you try to employ outworkers they insist that the regulations do not relate to them because they are self-employed or for some other reason. As explained below, unless they can show you a certificate confirming that they are registered as self-employed, then they are covered by the regulations, whatever they may claim. If they continue to refuse to accept the regulations, you can presume that they are trying to avoid tax and you should employ someone else. This can lead to a Catch 22 situation – by insisting on staying within the law you may find it difficult to take on outworkers. Nevertheless, be wary of being pushed into an illegal position. If you expect your business to grow, and therefore the use of outworkers to increase, it is sensible to follow the rules from the start. The illegal way will only lead to worry and problems and, possibly, serious trouble. Illegally paying someone a fiver once in a while to help you might not be considered a great wrong, but paying out £50 every week to outworkers would.

Employing your husband or wife

You do not need to issue a spouse with a contract of employment, but again you are responsible for deducting tax and National Insurance where appropriate.

Part-time employees

For employment law purposes, part-timers are people who are employed for less than 16 hours a week. Although part-timers do not need a contract of employment, you are responsible for deducting tax and National Insurance where appropriate.

Full-time employees

Anyone who is employed for more than 16 hours a week on a continuous basis counts as a full-time employee and must be given a contract of employment in writing within 13 weeks of starting to work for you. This contract should cover the following points:
name of employer and employee;
title of the job;
rate of pay and how it is calculated;
whether it is paid weekly or monthly;
normal hours of work;
holiday entitlement and holiday pay
provision for sick pay;
period of notice which employee is entitled to receive and obliged to give;
any disciplinary rules relating to the job;
grievance procedures.

Apprenticeships

The contract of someone taken on as an apprentice will in addition, require details of agreements covering study, including attendance at external courses. Bear in mind that there are special regulations concerning the employment of people under 18.

National Insurance and tax

The requirements for National Insurance contributions are quite simple. If you employ anyone, even if they are registered as self-employed, and pay them £43 or more per week or £186 or more per month (1989-90 figures), then you must deduct National Insurance Class 1 contributions and, in addition, pay an employer's contribution. The contributions are calculated on the basis of the earnings; your local DHSS office can supply the necessary tables, paperwork and information. Employers' NI contributions count as a business expenditure for tax purposes.

Tax is more complicated and if you plan to employ anyone you should contact your local tax office for advice. They will also supply the necessary paperwork and tax tables where required. If you employ anyone it is your duty to deduct income tax from their pay, where due, whether or not you have been told to do so by the tax authorities. If you do not you are liable, not the employee, and you could end up paying the tax which should have been deducted.

If you are employing someone on a part- or full-time basis and this is their only employment you should receive from them a Form P45 parts 2 and 3 which the employee's previous employer should have completed. This form gives details of the employee's tax code and pay to date. As the new employer, you should complete this in accordance with the instructions in part 2. Part 3 is then sent to the tax office and you should prepare a tax deduction card which you obtain from the tax office with full instructions.

If the employee does not have a Form P45, a Form P46 must be completed instead and also, if he or she is going to earn more than £50 a week, a Form P15 (coding claim). Details for the relevant procedures for deducting tax and paying it to the Inland Revenue are explained in the information you will receive from the tax office.

If you are employing someone on a part-time or casual basis and they have other employment, then they must either give you a copy of their form confirming they are registered as self-employed or fill in Certificate B of a Form P46. If they can provide a form, then you do not require to deduct tax or keep tax records but should pay them the full amount on receipt of an invoice. Otherwise you should deduct tax at the standard rate (30%) and keep a record of the name, address and payments made for each employee. If you are likely to employ a number of outworkers or casual/freelance workers, then you should seek the advice of your local tax office on how best to deal with this.

At the end of each tax year you will have to make appropriate returns to the tax office giving details of anyone employed (except those registered as self-employed), payments made to them and tax deducted.

If an employee leaves, you will have to issue a P45. This form details the employee's code number and the pay and tax deducted to date in that year. At the end of each tax year (April) you must issue each employee with a Form P60 which gives details of the pay and tax deducted for the year.

Every employee who works for you more than 16 hours a week and who has been employed by you continuously for 104 weeks or more must be given a written statement of your reasons for wanting to dismiss him/her.

You are also required to give one week's notice (or payment in lieu) to anyone who has been employed for four weeks or more and, after two years, one week's notice for every year of continuous employment. Anyone dismissed within two years of commencing employment is excluded from claiming unfair dismissal. Given that dismissal can be necessary even where only one person is employed, and given the complexities of the various Employment Acts, it is important to ensure that you obtain further information on this subject.

Insurance

If you employ staff, you are legally required to take out Employer's Liability Insurance which covers you against any claims by employees who in the course of their employment with you suffer an injury or contract a disease due to your alleged negligence.

Conditions of work

These are many regulations covering working conditions and you should investigate those which may relate to you, for example, the use of machinery or harmful materials. If you are considering renting, buying or converting a workshop and propose to take on staff, you should check that the premises will conform to the requirements of the Health and Safety at Work Act.

Other regulations you may need to be aware of include length of hours, minimum wage and the employment of young people.

Fixed term contracts

If you only need to employ someone to carry out a specific job or for a short period, it is best to employ them on a fixed term contract which states the period they are employed for. This will ensure that at the end of the period you have no commitments to them.

Recruitment

Make sure you know exactly what you want the person to do and that the job is accurately described in advertisements. The difficulties and cost of discharging staff make it imperative that you try and choose the right person. Knowing exactly what you require them to do will also help you to interview possible candidates and assess their previous experience. Check references as these are not always reliable; a telephone check can be more useful than a written reference as previous employers will often be more honest without the threat of a possible libel action which is always inherent in documents. Ensure that no-one is discriminated against because of sex, religion or race.

INFORMATION

Having your own information system is invaluable and it is worth getting into the habit of noting down any piece of information or address that may be useful in the future. A box file of information, perhaps broken down into sections for ease of reference, and an address book are key business tools. (Given the importance of address books, losing one can be a major disaster and it is therefore sensible to keep a duplicate copy at home.)

In addition to the specific organisations listed below, reference libraries can provide answers to queries, either directly or by pointing you in the direction of relevant publications. Colleges and other craftspeople can help with information or answers to specific problems, and local chambers of commerce, the small business unit of your local council and your local tourist office can also be worth approaching if you have a query relevant to them.

CRAFTS COUNCIL

12 Waterloo Place, London SW1Y 4AU (Tel: 01-930 4811)
The Council has an extensive information centre based at its London gallery. Information is available on full-time, part-time and short courses in the crafts, forthcoming craft fairs and markets, craft shops and galleries, guilds and societies, places to obtain craft materials and tools, and addresses of group workshops. The Council also has a selection of current and back copies of relevant craft publications available to personal callers. Housed at the information centre are the Council's Register of Craftspeople and a Slide Library.

The Crafts Council Register consists of a card index of makers, divided according to craft and county, and is open to all professional craftsmen and women. The Council receives many enquiries about craftspeople to undertake commissions, take part in exhibitions, etc. so it is worthwhile ensuring that you are included. The Slide Library contains over 18,000 slides showing the work of makers on the Selected Index, items from the Council's Collection, exhibitions and the work of grant recipients. Slides can be viewed at the London offices or hired by post for a nominal charge. Details on how to apply for inclusion in the Selected Index is available from the Council's Information Section.

The Crafts Council can also help with specific problems encountered in running a business or marketing work, and you should not hesitate to get in touch if you need help or advice.

REGIONAL ARTS ASSOCIATIONS/WELSH ARTS COUNCIL

Apart from offering grants, these bodies operate schemes which can help supplement your income; they include placements in schools, fellowships and residencies. You should seek information on these from your local RAA or, if you live in Wales, the Welsh Arts Council.

As these bodies are often consulted about exhibitions, public commissions, the stocking of craft shops, etc., it is important that you let them know you exist. Most associations have indexes of craftsmen and women within their region and you should ensure that you are included.

Buckinghamshire Arts 55 High Street Aylesbury HP20 1SA Tel: 0296 34704	Buckinghamshire
Greater London Arts 9 White Lion Street London N1 9PD Tel: 01-837 8808	32 London boroughs and the City of London
Eastern Arts Association Cherry Hinton Hall Cambridge CB1 4DW Tel: 0223 215355	Bedfordshire, Cambridgeshire, Essex, Hertfordshire, Norfolk, Suffolk
East Midlands Arts Mountfields House Forest Road Loughborough LE11 3HU Tel: 0509 218292	Derbyshire (except High Peak District), Leicestershire, Northamptonshire, Nottinghamshire and the borough of Milton Keynes
Lincolnshire & Humberside Arts St Hugh's 23 Newport Lincoln Tel: 0522 533555	Lincolnshire, Humberside
Merseyside Arts Graphic House Duke Street Liverpool L1 4JR Tel: 051 709 0671	Merseyside Metropolitan County, District of West Lancashire, Ellesmere Port and Halton districts of Cheshire
Northern Arts 10 Osborne Terrace Newcastle upon Tyne NE2 1NZ Tel: 091 281 6334	Cleveland, Cumbria, Durham, Northumberland and Tyne & Wear Metropolitan County

North West Arts 12 Harter Street Manchester M1 6HY Tel: 061 228 3062	Greater Manchester, Cheshire (except Ellesmere Port and Halton), Lancashire (except West Lancashire) and the High Peak district of Derbyshire
South East Arts 10 Mount Ephraim Tunbridge Wells TN4 8AS Tel: 0892 41666	East Sussex, Kent and Surrey
South West Arts Bradninch Place Gandy Street Exeter EX4 3LS Tel: 0392 218188	Avon, Cornwall, Devon, Dorset (excluding Bournemouth, Christchurch and Poole), Gloucestershire and Somerset
Southern Arts 19 Southgate Street Winchester SO23 7EB Tel: 0962 55099	Berkshire, Hampshire, Isle of Wight, Oxfordshire, West Sussex, Wiltshire and districts of Bournemouth, Christchurch and Poole
West Midlands Arts 82 Granville Street Birmingham B1 2LH Tel: 021 631 3121	Metropolitan County, West Midlands, Hereford, Worcester, Shropshire, Staffordshire and Warwickshire
Yorkshire Arts Glyde House Glydegate Bradford BD5 0BQ Tel: 0274 723051	South, West and North Yorkshire
(Wales) Welsh Arts Council (Craft and Design Dept.) 9 Museum Place Cardiff CF1 ENX Tel: 0222 394711	

DESIGN COUNCIL

28 Haymarket, London SW1Y 4SU (Tel: 01-839 8000)
The Design Council can advise on the solution to specific design problems, and provide information on relevant new technology.

BRITISH COUNCIL

10 Spring Gardens, London SW1A 2BN (Tel: 01-930 8466).
The British Council exists to promote wider knowledge of the UK and the English language abroad and to develop closer cultural relations between the UK and other countries. It organises British exhibitions touring abroad and can help craftspeople make contact overseas.

GOVERNMENT AGENCIES

Those listed on pages 8 and 9 also offer advice and information.

NATIONAL FEDERATION OF SELF-EMPLOYED AND SMALL BUSINESSES

(0253 720911)

A federation of around 50,000 members, operating mainly as a pressure group on behalf of small businesses. It can assist self-employed people with small commercial mortgages.

GUILDS & ASSOCIATIONS

There are a range of craft guilds, both national and regional, and all promote contact between craftspeople. All will help with information and a number assist in promoting and selling members' work. Before deciding to join any crafts body, check to see that it is relevant and of use. A list of all guilds is available from the Crafts Council's Information Section.

MAGAZINES

There are a number of specialist magazines; details can be obtained from the Crafts Council. The two magazines most relevant to all craftsmen and women are *Crafts* and *Artist's Newsletter.*

Crafts is bi-monthly, published by the Crafts Council, and it contains news, features on contemporary crafts, details of shops and galleries, forthcoming exhibitions, information on competitions, residencies, etc., and a useful advertisement section.

Artist's Newsletter is published monthly by Artic Producers, P.O. Box 23, Old Simpson Street School, Simpson Street, Sunderland SR4 6DG. It is an extremely useful magazine, concentrating on information for artists and craftspeople. This includes details of residencies, open exhibitions, awards etc., plus features on specific subjects such as publicising yourself, regional arts association grant schemes, commissioning, etc.

INDEX

NOTES